Environment
and
Religion

Dr. P. V .S. Vara Prasad
B.E(Civil).,M.Sc(Ecology&Env).,Ph.D.,M.Tech(Struct).,Ph.D.,

BlueRose ONE.com
Stories Matter
NewDelhi • London

BLUEROSE PUBLISHERS
India | U.K.

BlueRose ONE.com
Stories Matter
NewDelhi • London

For permissions requests or inquiries regarding this publication,
please contact:

BLUEROSE PUBLISHERS
www.BlueRoseONE.com
info@bluerosepublishers.com
+91 8882 898 898
+4407342408967

ISBN: 978-93-5819-628-3

Cover design: Muskan Sachdeva
Typesetting: Namrata Saini

First Edition: August 2023

Dedicated to my wife

Palla Lakshmi Kantham, B.A.,

ABOUT AUTHOR

I, Dr. Palla Venkata Sai Vara Prasad born on 22.08.1959 at Narasapuram, Christian Mission Hospital of West Godavari District , Andhra Pradesh. My primary education was completed in Government school at Pathuru village of Bhimadole mandal and the secondary school education was completed in Zilla Parishad High School at Bhimadole of west Godavari District.I Studied Diploma in Mechanical engineering from S.M.V.M.Polytechnic, Tanuku,W.G.Dt., during the year 1974-1977 and joined in Panchayat Raj Department, Government of Andhra Pradesh in the year 1978.

Further studied Diploma in Civil Engineering from S.M.V.M.Polytechnic, Tanuku in the year 1980 and studied B.E(Civil) fulltime from College Of Engineering, Pravaranagar, Loni, University of Pune (Maharastra State) during the year 1985-1988 while in Government service on study leave. Also completed my M.Sc (Ecology & Environment) from Sikkim Manipal university, in the year 2007 and pursued full time Doctor of Philosophy (Ph.D.,) in Civil Engineering from Monad University, Hapur of UP state and awarded in the year 2013.

I completed my M.Tech (structures) from Himalayan University, Itanagar, Himachal Pradesh and also completed my full time second Ph.D in Structural Engineering from OPJS University, CHURU of Rajasthan (INDIA) and awarded in the year 2021.

I served more than 32 years of Government service in Panchayat Raj Department, Government of Andhra Pradesh in various capacities and retired as Assistant Executive Engineer in the year 2019.Presently I am Director for V MOR HOLDINGS Pvt. Ltd., LUCKNOW and resident of Eluru town of Andhra Pradesh, India.

I am in academic field from the year 2010 to 2022 and worked as Professor and Principal in various Engineering Colleges. I taught various subjects like Environmental Engineering, Environmental studies, Air Pollution & Control, Environmental Impact Assessment, Concrete Technology, Pre-stressed concrete and Transportation Engineering to the Engineering students. My Passion is teaching and I used to educate the students with ethical, moral values and social life. **The main theme of bringing this book on "Environment & religion" is to create awareness among all the citizens in order to contribute their social responsibility towards protection of Environment and make clean country as well as clean world.**

Residential Address:

Flat No. 201, R.K.Platinum,

Gubbalavari street, R.R. Peta

Eluru – 534002, Andhra Pradesh, India

ACKNOWLEDGEMENTS

I submit that this research work on "Environment and Religion" has been dedicated at the Lotus feet of "Shirdi Sai Baba".

I would not bring out this luminous work without the blessings of my father late Sri Palla Adinarayana (Retired Head Master) and my mother Ratna Manikyam.

The role-played by my wife Lakshmi Kantham B.A., and my son Harish Jawahar, B.Sc (Tech-Marine)., M.Tech(thermal), 2nd Engineer, Marine., TORM Shippings Pvt Ltd..Mumbai in supporting me throughout my research work is worth mentioning.

And I place on record that my daughters namely Sravani palla B.E (civil)., MBA(Finance)., Chief Manager, ICICI Bank ,New Delhi and Sai Sowjanya Palla M.Pharm., Dy Manager Parexel International LLC. Bangalore, their encouragement, help and affection enable me to bring out this luminous work. I specially extend my heartful thanks to my daughter Sai Sowjanya Palla for formatting the book and also for their goodness.

I am also thankful for the advises received from my son-in-laws Mr. Ratnesh Shukla, MBA(Finance) - Banking and Dr.Pardha Saradhi Mathi, Ph.D(Bio-Technology), Senior Scientist -CMC, Evox Therapeutics Ltd., Oxford, United Kingdom are worth mentioning.

I specially express my deep sense of gratitude to all the authors whose papers and books mentioned in the reference of this book.

Dr. P.V.S.Vara Prasad,

B.E(Civil).,M.Sc (Ecology&Env).,Ph.D.,M.Tech(Struct).,Ph.D.,

THE ENVIRONMENT AND RELIGION PREFACE

Ancient Indian Mythology, the God prevails the whole universe. The cosmic vibrations, on Aum, structure all physical creation, including the human body, through the manifestation of "Five Tattwas" (elements): Earth, Water, Fire, Air and Ether. These are intelligent vibratory forces.

a.	*Without Earth element*	:	*There would be no state of solid matter*
b.	*Without Water element*	:	*There would be no liquid state*
c.	*Without Air element*	:	*There would be no gaseous state*
d.	*Without Fire element*	:	*There would be no heat*
e.	*Without Ether element*	:	*There would be no background on which Produce the cosmic motion picture show*

The four elements namely Water, Earth, Fire and Air are composed of our bodies. After we die the element of earth in our bodies will blend with the earth again, the breath will blend with the atmosphere again.

Religions, from ancient to modern times, which stem from the teachings of Philosophers, saints and sages such as Buddha, Jesus Christ, Mohammed, Confucius and Mencius, act as Guiding Light to inspire man towards moral awareness, the search for a truth within themselves, and the Law enshrined for nature and environmental harmony & conservation, and inspired the man to bestow reverence for the presence of Divinity in Nature.

Hinduism expresses the firm belief that God is omnipresent in various forms of Sky(Akasa), Air(vayu), Fire(tej),Water(jal), Earth(mother) and entities of plants(vana devata), and animals.

***RIG-VEDA** regarded plants as have Divine power. Accordingly, harm to plants, polluting Air, Water and Earth (land) shall regard as "SIN" as these were respected as God & Goddess.*

Religious leaders say that protecting the environment goes to the "heart of living the faith" and the environmental destruction is a sign of lost in moral bearings.

Today's environmental pollution problem is becoming larger in scale. This has caused undesirable changes in the physical, chemical and biological properties of land, air and water. Human mismanagement of natural resources, industrialization and agricultural development has given list to numerous environmental problems such as pollution of water, air, noise, degradation through deforestation and water logging that affected the human being. If this problem left unbridled, the problem may assume such from in immediate future, that life from the planet would totally be extinct.

Further, most of the developing countries including India have indulged in continued exploitation of the natural resources without seeing to its consequences. This has resulted into immense environmental pressure for future survival and development of people. Some environmental hazards have also come from natural events such as earthquakes, volcanoes, storms, etc. In India most of the population falls below the poverty line, in the absence of capital resources, the poor are dependent on the environment for their livelihood. For them, preservation and protection of environment may not be a prime concern resulting in large quantities of waste that released into the atmosphere. Indira Gandhi, the late Prime minister of India stated in Stockholm conference that 'poverty is the great Polluter'.

A brief concept about the pollution and its effects on all being and matters are also described here under to understand the need to bring out this book.

1.0 FORESTS & DEFORESTATION:

Forests are very important element in the structure of ecosystem. Forests are the global lungs, they influence climate, rainfall and regulate atmosphere. Forests functions are: water shed protection, erosion control by holding soil, and habitat for wild life as well as a land bank in maintaining soil nutrients and structure. However, they had great threat due to human activities and led to deforestation.

Forests are natural sink of carbon dioxide because they use carbon dioxide to prepare their food during the process of photosynthesis. In fact, forests are 'life line' of a nation because prosperity and welfare of the society directly depends on sound and healthy forest cover. Forests are main component of the biotic components of the natural environmental system and the stability of the environment and ecosystem/ecological balance largely depend on the status of the forests of region concerned. It is a matter of serious concern that in the present economic scenario man has forgotten the environmental and ecological significance.

Deforestation gives birth to several problems encompasses environmental degradation, soil erosion, increase in the sediment load of the livers, silting of reservoirs and river beds, increase in the frequency and dimension of floods and droughts, changes in the pattern of distribution of precipitation, intensification of greenhouse effects, increase in the destructive force of the atmospheric storms etc. Due to deforestation earth is becoming warmer; if this continues our earth will become a desert or will be covered with sea and will cause destruction of mankind.

The protection and conservation of forest resources are not only desirable but are also necessary for the economic development of a nation and maintenance of environmental and ecological balance from local through regional to global levels.

2.0 WATER, WATER POLLUTION & ITS EFFECTS:

Water is the most important element in the biosphere as "it is vital for the survival of all forms of life. 71% of the earth surface is covered by water. 97% of the total water available on earth is in Oceans and is saline. 3% of the total water available is fresh water. From this 3%, 2.997% located in ice caps.

Only, 0.003% of the earth's total volume of water is available to use as soil moisture ground water, water vapor and the water in lakes, streams, rivers and wetlands.

Fresh water becomes scarer the access to water resources will be an important factor in determining growth of several countries around the world.

In India, we use 90% of its water for agricultural purpose, 7% for industry and 3% for domestic use. A great challenge facing the World in this century is need to rhythmic the overall management of water resources. Through evaporation and precipitation, maintains hydrological systems, which form rivers and lakes, and supports a variety of aquatic ecosystem. A large number of people for their daily needs such as drinking water, washing, cooking watering animals and irrigated fields, uses all aquatic ecosystems.

The substances that degrade the quality of water are water pollutants. Water pollution is defined as alteration in physical, chemical (or) biological characteristics of water making it unsuitable for designated use in its natural state.

The water pollutant emanates from two basic sources namely (i) natural sources, and (ii) anthropogenic sources. The natural causes that contribute to water pollution are; includes soil erosion, deposition of dead and decaying remains of plants and animals, high-speed winds, floods and volcanic eruptions etc.

The anthropogenic sources are the real sources of water pollution. The anthropogenic sources of water pollution, like industrial waste, agricultural waste, sewage disposal, human activities, customs etc.

The water pollution can be assessed based on certain parameters, namely, (I) physical (ii) chemical and (iii) biological parameters. Physical parameters used to ascertain the quality of water include temperature, colour, odor, turbidity, conductivity, and density and suspended, dissolved and total solids. Chemical parameters include nature and amount of soluble salts, hardness of water, acidity and alkalinity of water, dissolved oxygen (Do), biological oxygen demand (BOD) chemical oxygen demand (COD), concentration of hydrogen ion (pH), amount of ammonia, nitrate and nitrites, amount of heavy metals, lead, and chromium. Biological parameters are bacteria; coli form M PN algae, viruses, etc.

EFFECTS OF WATER POLLUTION:

The effects of water pollution are varied and depend on the toxicity of the chemicals that dumped on the location of the site of disposal. Many water bodies near urban areas are highly polluted and cause several diseases in human beings and destroy aquatic ecosystems. The various effects of water pollution are:

2.1 EFFECTS ON HUMAN HEALTH:

Consumption of polluted water may lead to various diseases of the central nervous systems and may cause damage to the liver, brain and kidneys etc.

2.2 EFFECTS ON ANIMALS:

The organisms that live in aquatic habitats are directly affected by water pollution. The increase in amounts of pollutants in water, a large number of known and unknown aquatic plant and animal species have become extinct.

2.3 EFFECTS ON PLANTS:

Nitrate and phosphate fertilizers are used to increase the nitrogen and phosphate content of soil act as pollutants. Polluted water also contains a relatively high concentration of heavy metals, which may be toxic for plants and hence hamper their growth.

The long term and indirect effects of the prolonged presence of chemical pollutants in water bodies shall best illustrated by the "Minimata" episode of Japan.

2.4 AIR POLLUTION & ITS EFFECTS:

The Earth's atmosphere is a layer of gases that held together by Earth's gravity. Atmosphere forms a protective cover around the Earth. It contains a number of gases that are present in definite concentrations and ratios, and it regulates all the processes of Biosphere.

Exhausts from industries, emissions from automobile engines (carbon monoxide), combustion of fossil fuels (carbon dioxide), release of 'hydrocarbons' from vehicles, industries and refineries, are air polluters. And also Nitrogen oxides from power generators and forest fires, sulphur compounds including sulphur oxides, hydrogen sulphide from "biological decomposition- smelting of sulphide containing ores- combustion of sulphur-containing fuels such as coal and particulate matter are all responsible for "air pollution" and not only altering the ratio of gases, but also increasing the concentration of undesirable gases in the atmosphere.

There are more than 750,000 manmade chemicals present in our environment and to this, 1000-2000 new ones are added every year, and all the pollutants put together 2 billion tons of air pollutants are released every year.

The various natural sources of air pollution are dust storms, volcanic eruptions and bacterial activity of soil. The main artificial sources are industries, combustion, solid waste treatment and transportation. Pollutants generated by thermal power stations are fly ash, sulphur-di-oxide and other gases, and hydrocarbons and a nuclear explosion causes severe 'Air pollution'.

2.5 EFFECTS ON HUMAN HEALTH:

Air pollution has long-term and short-term effects on human health. Irritation of eyes, nose, throat and upper respiratory infections are short-term effects. Moreover, chronic respiratory diseases, lung cancer, heart diseases, damage to the brain, nerves, liver or kidneys are some of the long-term effects of Air pollution.

2.6 EFFECTSON PLANTS:

In plants, air pollution affects stomata movements, photosynthesis and growth. At high concentration of SO2, the amount of chlorophyll declines causing chlorosis of leaves. A very high concentration leads to the death of leaves. High concentration of NO2 leads to the development of 'Necrotic' spots. High concentration of CO leads to premature falling of leaves, smaller leaf size, curling, etc.

3.0 CLIMATE CHANGE AND ITS EFFECTS:

Increase in 'air pollution results in changes in "climatic" conditions and weather patterns. Climate change is a change in the statistical distribution of weather patterns when that change lasts for an extended period of time. Climate change may refer to a change in average weather conditions, or in the time variation of weather within the context of longer-term average conditions. Climate change is caused by factors such as biotic processes, variations in solar radiation received by Earth, plate tectonics, and volcanic eruptions. Certain human activities have been identified as primary causes of ongoing climate change, often referred to as global warming.

The global surface temperature increase by the end of the 21st century is likely to exceed 1.5 °C relative to the 1850 to 1900 period for most scenarios, and is likely to exceed 2.0 °C for many scenarios. Global mean sea level will continue to rise at a rate very likely to exceed the rate of the past four decades.

Climate models predict that Earth's global average ***temperature will rise*** *in the future. For the next two decades warming of about 0.2° Celsius is projected. If we continue to emit as many, or more, greenhouse gases, this will cause more warming during the 21st Century than we saw in the 20th Century. During the 21st Century, various computer models predict that Earth's average temperature will rise between 1.8° and 4.0° Celsius.*

Warmer average global temperature will cause a higher rate of evaporation, causing the water cycle to "speed up". More water vapor in the atmosphere will lead to more ***precipitation****. According to models, global average precipitation will most likely increase by about 3-5% with a minimum increase of at least 1% and a maximum increase of about 8%. Yet, changes in precipitation will not be evenly distributed. Some locations will get more snow, others will see less rain. Some places will have wetter winters and drier summers.*

A warmer climate causes ***sea level to rise*** *via two mechanisms: (1) melting glaciers and ice sheets (ice on land) add water to the oceans, raising sea level, and (2) ocean water expands as it warms, increasing its volume and thus also raising sea level. During the 20th Century, sea level rose about 10 to 20 cm (4 to 8 inches). Thermal expansion and melting ice each contributed about half of the rise, though there is some uncertainty in the exact magnitude of the contribution from each source. By the year 2100, models predict sea level will rise between about* ***20 and 50 cm*** *(8 to 20 inches) above late 20th Century levels. Thermal expansion of sea water is predicted to account for about 75% of future sea level rise according to most models.*

The ***2015 United Nations Climate Change Conference, COP 21 or CMP 11*** *was held in Paris, France, from 30 November to 12 December 2015. It was the 21st yearly session of the Conference of the Parties (COP) to the 1992 United Nations Framework Convention on Climate Change (UNFCCC) and the 11th session of the Meeting of the Parties (CMP) to the 1997 Kyoto Protocol. According to the organizing committee at the outset of the talks, the expected key result was an agreement to set a goal of limiting global warming to "well below 2 °C" Celsius compared to pre-industrial levels. The agreement calls for zero net anthropogenic greenhouse gas emissions to be reached during the second half of the 21st century. In the adopted version of the Paris Agreement, the parties will also "pursue efforts to" limit the temperature increase to 1.5 °C.The 1.5 °C goal will require zero emissions sometime between 2030 and 2050, according to some scientists.*

Global temperatures are likely to surge to record levels in the next five years, fueled by heat-trapping greenhouse gases and a naturally occurring El Niño. According to this report issued by the World Meteorological Organization, there is a 66% likelihood that the annual average near-surface global temperature between 2023 and 2027 will be more than 1.5°C above pre-industrial levels for at least one year. There is a 98% likelihood that at least one of the next five years, and the five-year period as a whole, will be the warmest on record. The Paris Agreement refers to the 1.5°C threshold for long-term warming over many years. This report predicts the level will be breached temporarily, with increasing frequency, but not permanently.

4.0 GREEN HOUSE EFFECT AND GLOBAL WARMING:

The layer of carbon dioxide gas present in the atmosphere acts as a greenhouse that allows heat to enter but prevents from radiating out. An increase in the concentration of CO2 causes accumulation of heat in the atmosphere shall known as "green house effect". The constant accumulation of heat leads to the phenomenon of 'Global warming' which refers to the increase in the average temperature of Earth and ultimately may cause the melting of ice caps and lead to a rise in Sea Level.

The latest IPCCC report warns that atmospheric levels of the three main greenhouse gases - carbon dioxide, methane, and nitrous oxide - reached new record highs in 2021, showing the biggest year-on-year jump in methane concentrations since systematic measurements began nearly 40 years ago. Moreover, the increase in carbon dioxide levels from 2020 to 2021 was larger than the average annual growth rate over the last decade.

5.0 ACID RAIN:

Gases such as sulphur dioxide and nitrogen oxides that emitted as wastes from industries react with atmospheric moisture, form sulphuric, and nitric acids. These acids mix with rainwater and reach the earth's surface as "Acid Rains".

The phenomenon of rain is caused when heat from the Sun's rays on the surface of seas, lakes and rivers induces evaporation. The water vapor formed in the process rises to a height where it condenses into moisture. If ambient conditions prevail it comes down as rain. But in the case of acid rain, water vapor reaches the atmosphere, condenses, and reacts with atmospheric gases like SO_2 and No_x. When it rains, these atmospheric pollutants are deposited on the soil, vegetation, surface water or reservoirs. The deposition ultimately results in damage because of the acidity of the pollutants.

India faces an increasing threat from acid rain -- earlier believed to be the scourge of the West. The large-scale industrial growth and reliance on the use of coal and crude oil distillates like diesel have led to acidification of the atmosphere. The burning of fossil fuels is mainly responsible for creation of Sulphur dioxide (SO_2) and oxides of nitrogen (No_x) which lead to the formation of acid rain. Automobile exhaust fumes are partly to blame, but the worst culprits are coal-burning thermal power plants and the steel industry. Already, a low pH has been observed at Chembur, Maharashtra and Delhi. This is the conclusion of a study conducted by Manju Mohan and Sanjay Kumar of the Centre for Atmospheric Sciences, Indian Institute of Technology (IIT), New Delhi.

6.0 DEPLETION OF OZONE LAYER:

Ozone is a triatomic molecule consisting of three atoms of Oxygen. It exists as gaseous form in the 'stratosphere' and is unstable. Ozone forms a protective shield of 24 km thickness in the stratosphere about 15 kms away from earth's surface and prevents the entry of 'ultraviolet' radiation on the Earth's surface where all being live. Its profile is shaped like that of earth, being highest at equator and lowest at the poles.

Chlorofluorocarbons (CFCs) and other halogenated ozone depleting substances (ODS) are mainly responsible for man-made chemical ozone depletion.

In nature, ozone is continuously formed and destroyed through photochemical interaction and equilibrium in ozone concentrations be ensured. Moreover, this equilibrium is upset due to the discharge of anthropogenic air pollutants such as CFCs, the chlorofluorocarbons, into the atmosphere. The CFCs release free radicals of chlorine, fluorine, or bromine, which destroy the stratospheric ozone as a result there is 'depletion of ozone'.

When CFCs reach the upper atmosphere, they are first degraded by the very high energy of UV (ultra-violet) radiation. Degradation of CFC leaves a free chlorine atom. The ***basic cause of ozone layer depletion is that this chlorine atom then breaks up ozone molecules****.*

Depletion of the ozone layer has consequences on humans, animals and plants. This typically results from higher UV levels reaching us on earth. Research confirms that high levels of UV Rays cause non-melanoma ***skin cancer****.*

7.0 NOISE POLLUTION & ITS EFFECTS:

The word 'noise' is derived from the 'Latin' word 'nausea' meaning 'seasickness'. It refers to a loud sound that may cause sickness. In physical terms, sound can be defined as a fluctuation in pressure in an elastic medium. The unpleasant and unwanted sound is called the 'noise'. High levels of noise that lead to discomfort and health hazards which is known as 'noise pollution'.

Since the last two to three decades, the amount of noise pollution in the environment has risen at an alarming rate. The natural phenomenon's that cause noise pollution are volcanic eruptions, thunder, fierce storms and apart from this, a rapid growth in human activities caused a severe increase in noise pollution.

8.0 EFFECTS OF NOISE POLLUTION

The effects of noise pollution classified as "Auditory effects and Non-auditory effects".

8.1 AUDITORY EFFECTS:

Exposure to high intensity sound even for a short duration can result in temporary deafness. Continuous exposure to high intensity noise will lead to irreversible loss, i.e., permanent deafness.

8.2 NON-AUDITORY EFFECTS:

They are effect on human health and effect on wild life.

EFFECTS ON HUMAN HEALTH:

The physical disorders due to anxiety, insomnia, high blood pressure, fatigue etc occur because of over-exposure to noise. Excessive noise levels leads to poor concentration and reduces the working efficiency. Regular exposure to loud noise may lead cause speech and reading disabilities in young children.

EFFECTS ON WILDLIFE:

Loud noise increases the rate of mortality by interfering with the delicate balance in the predator-prey detection and avoidance. Loud noise also cause stress in animals and many animals become dull and inactive and their health deteriorates due to continued exposure to high intensity.

The other pollutions that causing great harm to the environment are Soil pollution, Marine pollution, Thermal pollution, Radiation pollution and nuclear hazards etc.

9.0 CONCLUSIONS:

God has created this universe so wonderful and beautiful nature with abundantresources along with tremendous solar energy for better and sustainable living of all species. Man is a part of all living beings and can live happily and hopefully with peace and comfort, if there is harmony between God and environment. Therefore, it is necessary to manage and utilize resources without causing any damage to the environment.

Man is clever but not wise. Today man became greedy, and a tendency has been developed towards over exploitation and miss-management of natural resources, which lead to a serious threat of resources. This over exploitation and miss-management of natural resources had ultimately generated enormous wastes and led to great pollution to the environment.

*Today prevention of pollution is of paramount importance and every individual shall contribute sincere efforts towards decreasing pollution not only be visible at the community, city, state or national level but also at the Global level as a whole. Those who continue to cause environmental pollution should realize that they are harming the society of which they are a part. It is aptly said "***Think globally but act locally***" and develop an attitude that "***live and let live***" as nature's property is every one's (species) right and have equal right of utilization and as well as preservation and conservation.*

To achieve better environment by preventing pollution at all levels (prevention is better than cure), shall be possible through social values and ethical values of human beings. These values are associated with social life, customs, religion and psycho-spiritual aspects of the people.

The religious literatures, speeches of great saints & sages shall create strong sentimental feelings of human beings, which bring forth a healthy environment*. This healthy environment is possible through wide spread of the writings and messages of all religions feelings towards preservation and conservation of environment. Thus, this book has brought forward by highlighting the relationship between "***Environment and Religion***" to save and protect the Environment and make clean country as well as clean world.*

At the end of the entire chapter's index was given with meanings of more than 1000 words that help to understand easily.

CONTENTS

Chapter- 1

INTRODUCTION

1.1 Environment, 1.2. Environmental Pollution, 1.2.1. Air Pollution, 1.2.2. Water Pollution, 1.2.3. Soil Pollution, 1.2.4. Thermal pollution, 1.2.5. Radioactive Pollution, 1.2.6. Light pollution, 1.2.7. Visual pollution, 1.3. Science and Technology. 1.4 Anthropogenic Sources.

1.1 ENVIRONMENT:

"Environment"is the sum total of all social, economical, biological, physical, and chemical factors which constitute the surroundings of human, who are both the creators and moulders of the environment at a given point in space and time.

In the beginning, the environment of early man consisted of only physical aspects of the planet earth (land, air and water) and biotic aspects with march of time and advancement of society and man extended his environment through his social, economic and political functions. "Environment" includes water, air, land and the inter-relationship between both living organisms and non-living organism's i.e. both abiotic and biotic parts of nature.

Environment is the sum total of influences which modify and determine the development of life and its characteristics.

In fact environment is an inseparable and is constituted by the interacting; systems of physical and biological elements which are interlinked individually as well as collectively in many ways. Physical elements (space, landforms, water bodies, climate, soils, rocks and minerals) determine the variable character of the human habitat and its opportunities have limitation. Biological elements (plants, animals, microorganism and mass) constitute the biosphere.

Since the environment is both physical and biological concept, it encompasses both the non-living (abiotic) and living (biotic) components of the earth planet. The basic structure of the environment divided into two basic types, e.g. physical or abiotic environment and biotic environment. On the basis of physical characteristics and state, abiotic or physical environment is divided into three broad categories viz. (i) solid, (ii) liquid and (iii) gas, which represents the lithosphere (solid earth), the hydrosphere (water component) and the atmosphere respectively. Thus, the three basic divisions of physical environment may be termed as (i) lithosphere environment (ii) hydrosphere environment and (iii) atmospheric environment.

The biotic component of the environment consists of plants and animals including man as an important factor. Thus, the biotic environment divided into plants environment and animal's environment. All the organisms work to from their social groups and organizations at several levels and thus are formed social environment wherein the organisms work to derive matter from the physical environment for their sustainability and development.

Ecological approach to the study of man-environment relationship is based on the basic principle of study of mutual interactions between organism and physical environment on the one hand **and interactions among the organisms on the other hand in each ecosystem**. The stability of ecosystem refers to balance between production and consumption of each element in the ecosystem. In other words, ecosystem stability means balance between input and output of energy and normal functioning of different bio-geo-chemical cycles and stable conditions of concentration of all elements. Ecosystem instability refers to that state when an ecosystem is unable to adjust with environmental changes. These changes are conscious and enormous, and these changes exceed the resilience or capacity of the ecosystem.

For example: Rapid rate of felling of trees in a forest ecosystem seldom allows regeneration of forest community. Due to deforestation, the forest community often subjected to weathering, erosion, and nutrients washed out by surface run-off.

1.2 ENVIRONMENTAL POLLUTION:

Environmental pollution is a popular issue after World War II. It can be said that pollution is the result of our social development through the means of science. Pollution is the product of our scientific achievements being applied for the improvement of human facilities. Environmental pollution has become the biggest problem to the human race on this planet. Pollution is adding impurity to our environment; Pollution in our environment will hamper the core of existence of man and nature.

Environmental pollution means any solid, liquid or gaseous substances present in such concentration as may be, injurious to environment. Environmental pollution is a term that refers to all the ways by which people pollute their surroundings. People pollute the air with gases smoke, poison the water with chemicals and other substances and damage the soil with too many fertilizers and pesticides, which became a serious cause that the human being is facing today.

Environmental pollution is causing a lot of distress not only to humans but also animals, driving many animal species to endangerment and even extinction. The trans boundary nature of environmental pollution makes it even more difficult to manage it. It’s widely recognized that we are hugely overspending our current budget of natural resources – at the existing rates of its exploitation, there is no way for the environment to recover in good time and continue “performing” well in the future.

THE DIFFERENT TYPES OF POLLUTION ARE

- Air Pollution
- Water Pollution
- Soil Pollution
- Noise Pollution
- Radioactive Pollution
- Light Pollution
- Thermal Pollution
- Visual Pollution

1.2.1 Air Pollution:

It is caused by the release of chemicals and particulate matter into the atmosphere. Gaseous pollutants include carbon monoxide, sulphur dioxide, CFCs, nitrogen oxidesetc. Gaseous pollutants are usually produced by industry and motor vehicles. The main contributors for air pollution are human-made pollutants due to activities like combustion, construction, mining, agriculture and warfare are significant. Emissions from motor vehicles are one of the leading causes of air pollution.

India is not an exception, where majority of the population is exposed to poor air quality. India faces the similar challenges of both strengthening its economy and protecting its environment. Air quality has deteriorated in large cities in India. The major sources of air pollution include road dust re-suspension, diesel combustion, construction activities, biomass burning, certain contribution from gasoline which has polluted cities like Delhi, Mumbai, Kolkata, Chennai, Ankleshwar, Dhanbad, Howrah, Jharia, Surat, Jamshedpur, Sindri, Pune, Agra, Noida, Kanpur, Faridabad, Firozabad, Ghaziabad, etc.

Among other pollution sources, agriculture (livestock farming) is worth mentioning as the largest generator of ammonia emissions resulting in air pollution.

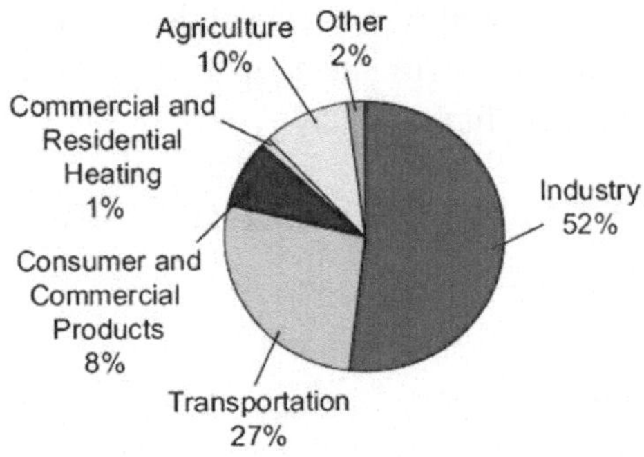

Fig:1

In order to control air pollution the following measurers are recommended which can have a positive impact to lessen the burden of economic cost.

- Use of CNG as fuel for processing /production.
- To replace DG sets with Gas generators.
- Restrict supply and usage of coal, coke, wood, rice husk, baggase to the industries situated in the city limit of Agra.
- All Petha Industries shall be operated by CNG/LPG only.

- Setting up of CNG/LPG retail outlets within Agra City for supplying CNG/LPG to the vehicles.
- Phasing out grossly polluting vehicles plying within the city.
- Checking for adulteration.
- Strict checking of vehicular emissions.
- Better traffic management.
- Construction paved footpaths / widening of roads up to the boundary limit along the major roads to minimize natural dust and congestion.
- Providing LPG for domestic and commercial use.

Air quality index (AQI) is a number used by government agencies to communicate to the public how polluted the air currently is or how polluted it is forecast to become. As the AQI increases, an increasingly large percentage of the population is likely to experience increasingly severe adverse health effects. Fine **particulate matter ($PM_{2.5}$)** is an air pollutant that is a concern for people's health when levels in air are high. $PM_{2.5}$ is tiny particles in the air that reduce visibility and cause the air to appear hazy when levels are elevated. **AQI: Good** (0 - 50) Air quality is considered satisfactory, and air pollution poses little or no risk. **AQI: Moderate** (51 - 100) Air quality is acceptable; however, for some pollutants there may be a moderate health concern for a very small number of people who are unusually sensitive to air pollution.

Index Value	Name	Color	Advisory
0 to 50	Good	Green	None
51 to 100	Moderate	Yellow	Unusually sensitive individuals should consider limiting prolonged outdoor exertion
101 to 150	Unhealthy for Sensitive Groups	Orange	Children, active adults, and people with respiratory disease, such as asthma, should limit prolonged outdoor exertion
151 to 200	Unhealthy	Red	Children, active adults, and people with respiratory disease, such as asthma, should avoid prolonged outdoor exertion; everyone else should limit prolonged outdoor exertion
201 to 300	Very Unhealthy	Purple	Children, active adults, and people with respiratory disease, such as asthma, should avoid outdoor exertion; everyone else should limit outdoor exertion
301-500	Hazardous	Maroon	Everyone should avoid all physical activity outdoors.

Fig:2

There are severe problems with both indoor and outdoor air pollution in India. The indoor air pollution is caused by many factors, but mostly the burning of toxic fuels to prepare meals. Indian people, burn coal, wood, and even animal dung to cook their meals, which releases toxins into the air they breathe. Breathing in this terrible quality air is responsible for nearly 500,000 deaths there each year.

This high number is mostly women and children and it is a serious problem. This number, according to the World Health Organization, is 80% of the nearly 600,000 deaths related to indoor air pollution in all of South East Asia. A shocking 70 percent of rural households in India do not have any ventilation at all. Air pollution in India caused by these problems could be cut in half by taking a few measures.

These measures include promoting smokeless cooking methods, and the use of proper ventilation. If these methods of helping were put into action then the deaths caused by indoor air pollution in India could be reduced by half.

1.2.2 Water Pollution:

Water pollution is the pollution or contamination of natural water bodies like lakes, rivers, streams, oceans, and groundwater due to inflow or deposition of pollutants directly or indirectly into water systems. Water pollution very often caused by human activities.

Any modifications or change in the chemical, physical and biological properties of water that can cause any harmful consequences on living things and the environment is known as water pollution.

Thermal water pollution is the rise or fall in water temperatures. These changes in the temperature of water can be caused due to industries. Some industries use water as cooling agent, the heated water is let-off directly into the natural environment at a higher temperature. Cold water pollution happens when cold water is released into the water bodies. Aquatic organisms like fish are vulnerable to slight changes in the temperature. Heated water decreases oxygen in the water killing fish and other aquatic organisms. Cold water affects eggs and larvae, some invertebrates of the aquatic ecosystem.

- Use of radioactive materials in nuclear plants meant for power generation
- The advent of nuclear medicines to cure and make arrange for precise diagnosis, with the help of radio isotopes
- Use of radio isotopes in industrial activities and various detectors
- Use of various radioactive derivatives to produce weapons of mass destructions
- Atomic waste materials and their subsequent disposal

Depending on the amount of radiation to which we are exposed and the sensitivity of each exposed person, the effects of radioactive pollution can vary significantly between individuals. However, any amount of radiation may cause cancer, and any exposure to radiation may cause some health risks. Effects of long, but low-intensity exposures include nausea, vomiting, diarrhea, loss of hair, bruises due to subcutaneous bleeding etc., Long-term exposure or exposure to high amounts of radiation can have far more serious health effects. When nuclear radiations and X-rays pass through genetic cells, they affect the chromosomes.

When the genetic cells are affected then the consequences are serious because the genes are affected i.e. mutation occurs. Tumors, cancer and developmental changes are other long-range effects of radiation pollution.

1.2.6 Light pollution:

Also known as photo-pollution. It is the presence of anthropogenic light in the night environment. This is exacerbated by excessive, misdirected or obtrusive uses of light, but even carefully used light fundamentally alters natural conditions. It is caused as a result of industrialization and modernization. It can be caused by various sources of light. The intrusive light falling inside our rooms from outside at night is a kind of light pollution called light trespass. Large industrial and residential areas cause light clutter. Any adverse effect of artificial light including sky glow, glare, light trespass, light clutter, decreased visibility at night, and energy waste.

Light pollution is unique as it is caused by man only. There is no comparable natural form of the pollution like there is with carbon dioxide. The main causes of light pollution are:

- **Poor Planning:** The placement of signage and street lights is planned by engineers, if they do not take into account the effect placement has on the surrounding environment they can create glare, light trespass and light clutter.
- **Irresponsible use** – You may love Christmas lights but leaving them on all night is a form of pollution, as is leaving a room with the lights still on or setting the timers on streetlamps and not adjusting the timer for the season. Not actively choosing to minimize energy waste is a huge source of light pollution.
- **Overpopulation** – That is really a zoning issue. Too many businesses, or too many residences, grouped in one area can cause light pollution of many kinds.
- **Animals** – Lights can attract or repel animals and insects. Most animal life functions on a diurnal or nocturnal system that is thrown out of sync by light pollution. This can place entire species in danger, or attract unwanted species into human areas.
- **People** – The wrong kind of light, or too much light has been proven to have an impact on your health and quality of life. Light pollution also increases danger to people as it can interfere with important navigational systems for trains, planes and even automobiles.
- **The Earth** – The Earth's ecosystem is dependent on cycles of natural light. Sky Glow alone can cause a loss in growth protection as the reflected light off the atmosphere will prevent the natural UV rays from reaching the Earth. This disrupts growth and decay cycles that our food, air and water supply is dependent on. Light pollution is not only a hindrances to astronomy, but it also impacts us directly. Light pollution has a wide range of negative effects on human health such as disrupting our circadian rhythms, messing with our melatonin levels, and generally contributing to sleeping disorders. Reduction or elimination of light at night can help maintain a robust melatonin rhythm.

Here are five ways you can reduce light pollution and help preserve Dark Skies in your area of the world.

- Use Core Glow stones for all your Outdoor Night Lighting: ...
- Only purchase IDA Approved light fixtures: ...
- Talk to your local representatives and support Dark Sky initiatives: ...
- Set an example - Turn your lights off!

1.2.7 Visual pollution:

It is an aesthetic issue and refers to the impacts of pollution that impair one's ability to enjoy a vista or view. Visual pollution disturbs the visual areas of people by creating harmful changes in the natural environment.

The primary sources of visual pollution are:

- Haze due to dust and air pollution
- Garbage heaps and landfills
- Telecommunication and electric wires and poles
- Signboards
- Barren lands and deforestation
- Urban Jungle- House constructed with bad design
- Smoke spewing chimneys of factories
- Graffiti

Effects of visual pollution:

1. Accidents:
    a. A building that is made entirely of glass can reflect sunlight, which is dangerous for the people driving by
    b. Billboards and advertisements on highway roads can distract drivers and cause accidents.
2. Depression, Stress and Anxiety due to bad views
3. Loss of tourism income
4. Crime- Studies show lower crime rate in areas with less visual pollution

Prevention:

There are two basic approaches to solving visual pollution – planning and education. Though it is difficult to change habits with people and expensive to redesign and replace what already exists.

1. Planning to create harmonious and peaceful surroundings
2. Education: The more people understand the importance of beautiful surroundings, the faster change will be seen.

1.3 SCIENCE AND TECHNOLOGY:

Science and technology brought in revolutionary change in human life. Modernization made man's life more and more comfortable. Today one can travel fast, speak, or send message to distant lands through the modern means of communication. Villages have become growing cities because of industrialization, which in turn presents its own side effects. Modern industries produce industrial wastes and toxic gases, which are hazardous to human health. The human being is exposed to air pollution, water pollution, soil pollution etc. in and around because of industrial wastes and the toxic gases from industry. Discovering new ways to use technology to reduce greenhouse gas emissions and manage resource consumption, in a way that is good for the economy, good for communities and good for the environment. A growing population means increased demand on our transport systems, healthcare services, and utilities.

While technology is blamed for much of the pollution that contributes to global warming, it may also provide the solution to the problem. Research into new methods of generating power and electricity is abundant; experts hope to find cleaner, renewable sources of energy to replace the finite supply of fossil fuels and reduce global warming and climate change. New methods such as wind turbines, solar power and hydro-electric power are under scrutiny and are constantly subject to trails to improve the efficiency of existing systems. The technological fix to environmental problems, will consist on improving ways in decreasing pollution. In research conducted at the University of Calgary, climate change scientist David Keith and a team of researchers showed it is possible to reduce carbon dioxide , which is the main greenhouse gas that contributes to global warming – using a relatively simple machine that can capture the trace of carbon dioxide present in the atmosphere at any place on the planet.

Any technology whose use is less environmentally harmful than alternatives is called an environmental technology. Wind turbines, solar panels and wave machines are environmentally friendly because they use renewable energy sources. Technologies that improve our environment are also included in this definition. Examples here include waste-management systems; recycling and clean transport systems that make use of fuel cells, hybrid engines or biofuels. Sustainable construction is also included. Houses can be built from environmentally friendly materials or built so that they do not produce pollution. Such a house is called a passive house. Information and Communications Technology (ICT) can also help as it can be used to improve energy use or reduce pollution from industrial processes.

Every day, new research is being conducted to improve the systems involved in the modern world. New systems of removing waste and improving the efficiency of the distribution of electricity, for example, may benefit many people in the future by cutting emissions and improving efficiency. Projects such as those involving cars that run on cleaner fuels may also significantly change the way we live in the future; energy efficient products such as light bulbs will also contribute to making the environment cleaner.

One of the principal reasons behind the significant gap between the developing world and the developed world is a lack of technology. The developed world is heavily reliant on technology which makes life much easier and production much more efficient. Technology is lacking in developing countries and this contributes to widespread poverty and a lack of basic amenities such as clean, running water and food supplies.

New technology which will boost food production, improve infrastructure, improve healthcare and provide sanitation facilities could dramatically change the quality of life in the developing world. With the help of charitable organizations and Government leaders from developed countries, this kind of technology is gradually being introduced into developing countries.

1.4 ANTHROPOGENIC SOURCE:

Anthropogenic source of pollution is varied and is the main culprit of environmental pollution. Anthropogenic source of pollution includes (a)Industrial source (b) urban source (c) agricultural source (d) Transport, e) pollution Source etc. Most of the pollutants come from industrial and urban sectors.

The industrial source: contributes many pollutants such as gaseous pollutants (nitrogen oxide, sulphur dioxide, carbon monoxide, hydrocarbon as methane and numerous toxic gases). Solid pollutants dissolved and suspended solids, wastewater having numerous chemical ingredients, heat, etc. During combustion processes in energy and transformation industries, or in manufacturing industries, the emissions depend on the fuel and process activity. Relevant pollutants are generally CO_2, H_2O, SO_2, NO_x, CO, NMVOC, aerosol particles, heavy metals (HM), polycyclic aromatic hydrocarbons (PAH), polychlorinated dibenzo-dioxin and polychlorinated dibenzo-furans (PCDD/F) and, for some activities, polychlorinated biphenyls (PCB) and hexachlorobenzene (HCB) During the combustion of coal, particles undergo complex changes, which lead to vaporization of volatile elements. The rate of volatilization of heavy metal compounds depends on fuel characteristics (e.g., concentrations in coal, fraction of inorganic components, such as calcium) and on characteristics of technology (e.g. type of boiler, operation mode).

Urban sourcesof pollution contribute sewage water, solid waste gaseous exhaust, liquid effluents, pollutants coming out of chimneys of factories located within the urban centers, etc., The two main causes of pollutants in urban areas are transportation technologies such as the automobiles and power production technologies such as industrial heating and cooling and coal-burning power plants. Automobiles produce a large amount of carbon monoxides to the air we breathe in.

Agricultural source of pollution includes the pollutants related to chemical fertilizers, pesticides and insecticides. Main sources of emission from animal husbandry and manure management are livestock housing and holding areas, manure storage, field-applied manure and manure deposited during grazing. During these activities NH_3, NO and NMVOCs are emitted to the atmosphere. Additionally, livestock feeding is another source of particles.

Main sources of crop production and agricultural soils are fertilizer application (NH3), soil microbial processes (NO) crop processes (NH_3 and NMVOCs) soil cultivation and crop harvesting (PM).

An additional, less important agricultural source of air pollutants is crop burning. During these processes ammonia (NH_3), nitrogen oxides (NO_x), non-methane volatile organic compounds (NMVOCs), sulphur dioxide (SO_2), carbon monoxide (CO), particulate matter (PM), heavy metals (HM) and dioxin are released to the atmosphere.

Transport: Transport is another major source of air pollutants. Terrestrial, naval and aerial transportation use a huge amount of energy and during the combustion processes, various components are emitted into the atmosphere. In order to comply with emission legislation, vehicle manufacturers have installed various after-treatment devices, such as catalytic converters and diesel particle filters (DPFs) to reduce pollutant emissions. However, such devices may, as a result of their action, also produce small quantities of pollutants such as NH_3 and N_2O.

During terrestrial transport, the most important pollutants emitted by road vehicles are ozone precursor compounds, (CO, NOx, NMVOCs), greenhouse gases (CO_2, CH_4, N_2O), acidifying substances (NH_3, SO_2), aerosol particles, carcinogenic species, such as polycyclic aromatic hydrocarbons (PAHs) and persistent organic pollutants (POPs), heavy metals and other toxic substances (dioxins and furans).

The emissions produced by railways arise from combusting the fuel in an internal combustion engine. Consequently, the principal pollutants are those from diesel engines, i.e. similar to those used in road transport.

These are principally CO_2, PM and NOx, plus to a lesser extent CO and hydrocarbons, together with SO_x and heavy metals originating from the content of fuel in sulphur and metals, respectively.

The emissions produced by aviation come from the use of jet fuel (jet kerosene and jet gasoline) and aviation gasoline (used to fuel small piston engine aircraft only) that are used as fuel for the aircraft. Consequently, the principal pollutants are those common to other combustion activities, i.e., CO_2, CO, hydrocarbons and oxides of nitrogen, with SO_2 emissions being dependent of the level of sulphur in the fuel. Other important species (like PM, N_2O, CH_4) are emitted at relatively low concentrations. Air pollutants emitted by aircrafts can affects the atmospheric processes in the free troposphere and in the lower stratosphere too.

Water-borne navigation causes emissions of carbon dioxide (CO_2), methane (CH_4) and nitrous oxide (N_2O), as well as carbon monoxide (CO), non-methane volatile organic compounds (NMVOCs), sulphur dioxide (SO_2), particulate matter (PM) and oxides of nitrogen (NOx).

Current anthropogenic emissions of CO_2 are primarily the result of the consumption of energy from fossil fuels. About 20–33% of total anthropogenic sources of methane (CH_4) is also originated from combustion.

Pollution source: pollution can take the form of chemical substances or energy, such as noise, heat or light. Pollutants, the components of pollution, can be either foreign substances/energies or naturally occurring contaminants. Pollution is often classed as point source or nonpoint source pollution. Anthropogenic (man-made) pollution is caused due to man-made sources or by human activities. Burning of fossil fuels, deforestation, mining, sewage, industrial effluent, pesticides, fertilizers etc. can cause anthropogenic pollution. A point source of pollution is a single identifiable source of air, water, thermal, noise or light pollution. A point source has negligible extent, distinguishing it from other pollution source geometries Nonpoint source pollution can include: Excess fertilizers, herbicides and insecticides from agricultural lands and residential areas etc.,

The responsibility of humans regarding the dispersion of aerosols and PHTEs (Polyurethane Hypericum Perforatum Extract) by anthropogenic activities is undeniable, but mankind also holds a strong responsibility in the intensification of natural dispersal processes. For example, the burning of biomass, i.e., forest fires, have been naturally occurring as a part of plant development and ecological renewal for more than 400 million years, yet these fires are now mainly driven and controlled by humans (Andreae and Rosenfeld, 2008). Similarly, desertification of semiarid lands and the intensification of agriculture on bare soil also helps to accelerate the natural suspension of dust (Rauch and Pacyna, 2009) and thus also the dispersal of PHTEs (Polyurethane Hypericum Perforatum Extract).

Human population is the most important source of pollution because all forms of anthropogenic pollution are the creation of human activities.

On an average, the increase in the population of a nation has positively correlated with pollution. The ever increasing population in the developing countries is posing as much as problem of population in the developing countries through industrial growth and urban expansion. Poverty and underdevelopment are yet other sources of pollution.

****

Chapter- 2

Religion & Environment Protection

2.1 RELIGION AND ENVITRONMENT PROTECTION:

Religion is commonly pertains to the spiritual domain while the science and technology are viewed as a system pertaining to the material domain. Issue of material development and progress therefore, been left to the change of scientific experts while religious belief has been left to guide the inner spiritual development of the individuals. The ecological crisis in the ultimate analysis can lead to the undermining of very basis of material existence.

The paradoxical situation in which rapid scientific and technological change has been associated with rapid destruction of the material basis of life, poses the most critical challenges of our times. This challenge creates two situations. On the one hand, it allows the reappraisal of religious and cultural beliefs as social systems for ordering the material and secular world. On the other hand, it allows the reappraisal of scientific beliefs in terms of their adequacy in knowing nature's patterns, rhythms and relationship in order to maintain them ecologically.

It is obvious that Indian and cultural traditions are very rich and rivers in values. These include all the major religions. Religious traditions and beliefs in India played a vital role in protection of environment. The earliest religious thought of India is **'Rig-Veda'**, which itself begin with a vivid description of five elements i.e., earth. Air, water, energy and space, which constitute our universe and gives the life support for man, animal and is the base for human activity and vegetation.

All major religions view that man is only among many creatures to enjoy nature's beauties and bounties. Nature has given him in trust to make wise and responsible use of it. NO religion justifies the destructive attitude of modem man, which has developed toward his environment.

Indifferent languages, different symbols, that all religions treat "**nature's God given gift**", some even state that God is omnipresent in the manifestations of nature.

2.2 SOURCES OF POLLUTION:

India has very rich tradition of concern for and protection of environment. The environment includes all parts of nature necessary for health and happiness of man. Nature reserves immense potential to maintain ecological balance. Not only the beauty but also the very existence of life depends on nature. The famous hymn in the world's oldest scripture, the Rig Veda portrays the beauty of the morning (ushas) and worships its glory. Our ancestors were worshiping the five elements of nature (Fire, Air, Earth, Sky and Water) as 'Panchabutas', because worship was a form of the greatest admiration for them in nature.

It is depressing to note that the water we drink and the air we breathe are polluted. We are now facing the serious ecological crisis like **acid rain, global warming, water and air pollution, the extinction of numerous animal and plant species, the loss of bio-diversity and ozone depletion**. The depletion of the Ozone Layer causes skin cancer, cataracts, damage to body's immunity system, mutation, loss of crop productivity and upsetting the balance of eco-systems. The need of the day is therefore to bring greater awareness for harmonizing population dynamics and socio-economic development and harnessing of natural resources with due care to see that the quality of the environment does not deteriorate.

2.2.1 GLOBALWARMING:

Global warming is when the Earth heats up (the temperature rises). It happens when green house gases (carbon dioxide, water vapor, Nitrous oxide and methane) trap heat and light from the Sun in the earth's atmosphere, which increases the temperature. This hurts many people, animals, and plants. Many cannot take the change, so they die. Of the total amount of greenhouse gasses, in agricultural production occurs about 30%. Thereof agricultural soil produce 32%, livestock 31%, crops cultivation 12%, from manure management occur 6% and 19% of other emissions. Specifically, gases released primarily by the burning of fossil fuels and the tiny particles produced by incomplete burning trap the sun's energy in the atmosphere. Scientists call these gases "greenhouse gases" (GHGs) because they act like the wrong way reflective glass in our global greenhouse.

Atmospheric gases like carbon-dioxide, methane, nitrous oxide, water vapour, and chlorofluorocarbons are capable of trapping the out-going infrared radiation from the earth. Infra-red radiations trapped by the earth's surface cannot pass through these gases and to increase thermal energy or heat in the atmosphere. Thus, the temperature of the global atmosphere is increased. As this phenomenon of increase in temperature is observed in green houses, in the botanical gardens these gases are known as green house gases and the heating effect is known as green house effect. If greenhouse gases are not checked, by the turn of the century the temperature may rise by 50°C. This will melt the polar ice caps and increase the sea level leading to coastal flooding, loss of coastal areas and ecosystems like swamps and marshes, etc.

Fig.3: Effect of Global Warming on Atmosphere

Fig. 4: Effect of Depletion of Ozone Layer on Earth

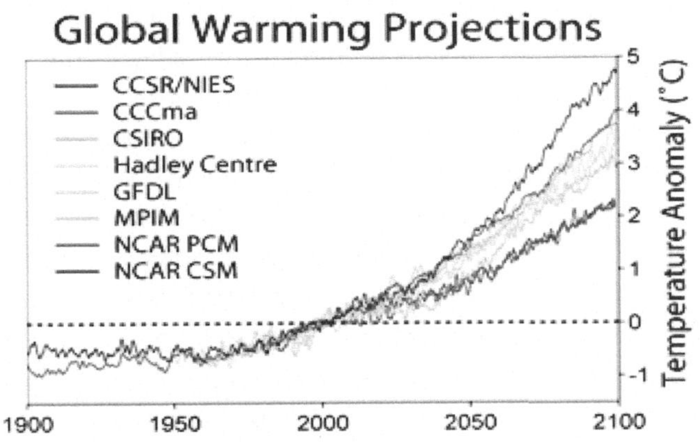

Fig.5: Graph Showing the Depletion of Ozone Layer

Fig.6: Image for global warming (industries)

Groups of scientists have recently reported on the surprisingly speedy rise in the discharge of carbon and methane release from frozen tundra in Siberia, now starting to melt because of human cause increases in earth's temperature. The scientists tell us that the tundra is in danger of melting holds an amount of extra global warming pollution that is equivalent to the net amount that is previously in the earth's atmosphere.

Likewise, earlier one more team of scientists reported that the in a single year Greenland witnessed 32 glacial earthquakes between 4.6 and 5.1 on the Richter scale. This is a disturbing sign and points that a huge destabilization that may now be in progress deep within the second biggest accretion of ice on the planet. This ice would be enough to raise sea level 20 feet worldwide if it broke up and slipped into the sea. Each day passing brings yet new proof that we are now in front of a global emergency, a climate emergency that needs instant action to piercingly decrease carbon dioxide emissions worldwide in order to turn down the earth's rising temperatures and avoid any catastrophe.

Fig.7: Melting of Ice Landscapes Due to Depletion of Ozone Layer

Fig.8: Melting of Ice Landscapes Due to Depletion of Ozone Layer

As the concentration of greenhouse gases grows, more heat is trapped in the atmosphere and less escapes back into space. This increase in trapped heat changes the climate and alters weather patterns, which may hasten species extinction, influence the length of seasons, cause coastal flooding, and lead to more frequent and severe storms.

Global warming is not only a threat to our future health, but it also already contributes to more than 150,000 deaths and 5 million illnesses annually, according to a team of health and climate scientists at the World Health Organization and the University of Wisconsin at Madison—and those numbers could double by 2030.

Research data published in the journal Nature show that global warming may affect human health in a surprising number of ways: speeding the spread of infectious diseases such as malaria and dengue fever; creating conditions that lead to potentially fatal malnutrition and diarrhea; and increasing the likelihood of heat waves and floods.

"The political resolve of policymakers will play a big role in harnessing the man-made forces of climate change," said Patz, who also holds a joint appointment with the UW-Madison department of Population Health Sciences. To reduce the demand for fossil fuels, that in turn reduces global warming, by using energy more wisely.

TEN SIMPLE ACTIONS THAT CAN HELP TO REDUCE GLOBAL WARMING:

1. Reduce, Reuse, And Recycle:

To reduce waste can be done by choosing reusable products instead of disposables. Buying products with minimal packaging (including the economy size when that makes sense for you) that helps to reduce waste. Moreover, recycle paper, plastic, newspaper, glass and aluminum cans reduces waste. By recycling half of the household waste can save 2,400 pounds of carbon dioxide annually.

2. Use - Less Heat and Air Conditioning:

Adding insulation to the walls and attic, and installing weather stripping or caulking around doors and windows can lower heating costs more than 25 percent, by reducing the amount of energy that needed to heat and cool the home.

Turn down the heat while sleeping at night or away during the dayand always keep temperatures moderate. Setting thermostat just 2 degrees lower in winter and higher in summer could save about 2,000 pounds of carbon dioxide each year.

3. Change a Light Bulb:

Wherever practical, replace regular light bulbs with compact fluorescent light (CFL) bulbs. Replacing just one 60-watt incandescent light bulb with a CFL will save Rs.125/-over the life of the bulb. CFLs also last 10 times longer than incandescent bulbs, use two-thirds less energy, and give off 70 percent less heat.

If every U.S. family replaced one regular light bulb with a CFL, it would eliminate 90 billion pounds of greenhouse gases, the same as taking 7. 5 million cars of the road.

4. Drive Less and Drive Smart:

Less driving means fewer emissions. Besides saving gasoline, walking and biking are great forms of exercise. Explore the community to mass transit system and check out options for carpooling to work or school.

When driving a car make sure that the car is running efficiently. For example, keeping tires properly inflated can improve gas mileage by more than 3 percent. Every gallon of gas saving not only helps the budget; it also keeps 20 pounds of carbon dioxide out of the atmosphere.

5. Buy Energy-Efficient Products:

When it is time to buy a new car, choose one that offers good gas mileage. Home appliances now come in a range of energy-efficient models, and compact florescent bulbs are designed to provide more natural-looking light while using far less energy than standard light bulbs. Avoid products that come with excess packaging, especially molded plastic and other packaging that cannot be recycled. If the household garbage reduced by 10 percent, that can save 1,200 pounds of carbon dioxide annually.

6. Use- Less Hot Water:

Set water heater at 120 degrees to save energy and wrap it in an insulating blanket if it is more than 5 years old. Buy low-flow showerheads to save hot water and about 350 pounds of carbon dioxide yearly. Wash clothes in warm or cold water to reduce the use of hot water and the energy required to produce it.

That change alone can save at least 500 pounds of carbon dioxide annually in most households. Use the energy-saving settings on dishwasher and let the dishes air-dry.

7. Use the "Off" Switch:

Save electricity and reduce global warming by turning off lights when leave a room and use the light as required. In addition, remember to turn off television, video player, stereo and computer when not using them.

It is also a good idea to turn off the water when not using it. While brushing teeth, shampooing the dog or washing your car, turn off the water until actually needed it for rinsing. Reduce water bill and help to conserve a vital resource.

8. Plant a Tree:

To plant a tree, start digging. During photosynthesis, trees and other plants absorb carbon dioxide and give off oxygen. They are an integral part of the natural atmospheric exchange cycle here on Earth, but there are too few of them to fully counter the increases in carbon dioxide caused by automobile traffic, manufacturing and other human activities. A single tree will absorb approximately one ton of carbon dioxide during its lifetime.

9. Get a Report Card from Your Utility Company:

Many utility companies provide free home energy audits to help consumers identify areas in their homes that may not be energy efficient. In addition, many utility companies offer rebate programs to help pay for the cost of energy-efficient upgrades.

10. Encourage Others to Conserve:

Share information about recycling and energy conservation with friends, neighbors and co-workers, and take opportunities to encourage public officials to establish programs and policies that are good for the environment.

These 10 steps will take a long way toward reducing your energy use and monthly budget. In addition, less energy use means less dependence on the fossil fuels that create greenhouse gases and contribute to global warming.

2.3 FACTORS OF ENVIRONMENTAL PROBLEMS:

Environmental factor or ecological factor or eco factor is any factor, abiotic or biotic, that influences living organisms. Abiotic factors include **ambient temperature, amount of sunlight, and pH of the water soil** in which an organism lives.

Examples of environmental factors include soil, water, climate, natural vegetation and landforms. Environmental factors entail everything that changes the environment. Some factors are visible, while others cannot be seen. In some situations, only the effects of environmental changes are evident.

"**Environmental crisis**" arises due to environment and ecological changes in the process of "**economic and technological strategiesin the present century**". In fact, if the present century marked by socio-economic, scientific and technological development on the one hand, and is plagued by serious problems of environmental problems on the other hand.

The environmental crisis arising out of the environmental deterioration caused by several forms of pollution, depletion of natural resources and rapid rate of their exploitation. Increasing dependence on energy consuming and ecologically damaging technologies, the loss of habitats due to industrial, urban and agricultural expansion, reduction and loss of ecological populations due to excessive use of toxic pesticides and herbicides and loss of several species of plants due to practice of monoculture removal of habitats through forest clearance has now become of global concern. The life of common person adversely affected by environmental degradation caused by man himself that there has been a marked growth of interest within the last decade in the quality of the environment, the disruption of the earth's natural ecosystems and the depletion of resources.

The most striking reason of the environmental degradation and hence global environmental crisis is the fact of deteriorating relationship between man and environment because of rapid rate of exploitation of natural resources, technological development and industrial expansion. The rate of environmental change and resultant environmental degradation caused by human activities has been so fast and widespread. The impact of man on environment through his economic activities are varied and highly complex as the transformation or modification of the natural condition and process leads to a series of changes in the biotic and abiotic components of the environment.

The impacts of man on environment fall into two categories (1) direct or intentional impacts and (2) indirect or unintentional impacts. Direct or intentional impact of human activities are preplanned, because man is aware of the consequences, both positive and negative of any program which is launched to change or modify the natural environment for economic development of the region concerned. The effects of anthropogenic changes in the environment are noticeable within short period and these effects are reversible. On the other hand the indirect impacts of human activities on the environment are not premeditated and preplanned and these impacts arise from those human activities which are directed to accelerate the pace of economic growth, especially industrial development. The indirect impacts can experience after long time when they become cumulative. This indirect effect of human economic - activities may change the overall natural environmental system and the chain-effects sometimes degrade the environment to such a labeled as the major source of environmental degradation.

2.3.1 DEFORESTATION:

Forests are invaluable property of a nation because they provide raw materials to modern industries, timber for building purposes, habitats for numerous types of animals and microorganisms. Good fertile and nutrient-rich soils having high content of organic matter, offer protection to soils by binding the soils through the network of their roots and by protecting the soils from direct impact of falling raindrops. They encourage and increase infiltration of rainwater and thus allow maximum recharge of groundwater resources, minimize surface run-off and hence reduce the frequency, intensity and dimension of floods. They help in increasing the precipitation; they are natural sink of carbon dioxide because they use carbon dioxide to prepare their food during the process of photosynthesis. They provide firewood to millions of people an over the world and food and shelter to innumerable humans and animals. In fact, forests are 'lifeline' of a nation because prosperity and welfare of the society directly depends on sound and health forest cover of a nation concerned have marked to accelerate the rate of soil loss through rains, sheet wash, rill and gully erosion, led to drought due to decrease in precipitation etc.

Forests are main component of the natural environmental system, the stability of the environment, ecological balance of the region concerned. A serious concern is that man has forgotten the environment and ecological significance of natural vegetations mainly forests and grasslands. The forests may often subjected to rapid destruction and pose the serious problems at global, regional and local levels which

From ecological point of view, at least one third of the total geographical area of country should be under rich forest cover but this general rule of environmental significance has flouted in many of the countries. Deforestation has immediate adverse effects on soils and land because of exposure of ground surface to high intensity of rainfall.

The major causes of deforestation at global and regional level are conversion of forestland into agricultural land, shifting cultivation, transformation of forests into pastures, overgrazing, forest fires, lumbering, multipurpose river projects etc.

Deforestation led to environmental degradation through accelerated rate of soil erosion, increase in the sediment load of the rivers, silting reservoirs and riverbeds. Changes in the pattern of distribution of precipitation, intensification of greenhouse effects causes atmospheric storms. Economic loss is due to, damages of agricultural crops with increased incidence of floods and draughts, decrease in agricultural production with loss of fertile top soils, decrease in the supply of raw materials to the industries and building construction etc. Thus, deforestation cause a chain effects which adversely affect the natural environment.

Forests are valuable and ecological assets. They protect land and Water resources and control floods and wind erosion, store and cycle nutrients and provide habitat for wildlife. Economically, forests provide energy, wood products, food, fodder, medicinal products and non-wood products such as fibers, rubber, gum and resins. Growing population has led to a disastrous over use and clearance of forests for fuel, timber, pulp and the paper industry.

Wood used as fuel leading to tremendous loss of forest cover. In Himachal, 3,000 square kilometer of forestland has damaged during the past 40 years. According to a study, the tropical forests are shrinking by eleven million hectares a year. The extensive loss of forest has serious economic and ecological implications.

Deforestation has caused carbon-dioxide concentration of the earth's atmosphere to rise from 290 to 350 microlitres per liter leading to global warming (greenhouse effect).

Fig.9: Image of Deforestation

Fig. 10:

Fig. 11: Image of Deforestation

The felling of forests disrupts the habitually wildlife and may lead to extinction of species. Species extinction may lead to a loss of an entire chain of dependent species and hence a loss of genetic diversity which is essential for survival and evolution in the long tern. The Botanical survey of India (1980) and the Zoological survey of India estimated that 4500 plant species and 75000 animal species in our country out of which 70 species of mammals 44 of birds, 15 of reptiles, 3 of amphibians and nearly 150 , plants species were found to be on the verge of extinction.

2.3.2 TECHNOLOGICAL DEVELOPMENT:

In recent years, the environmental crisis has closely related to the productive technology. The irony of the situation is that more the economic and industrial development in the world, the more is the danger to the environment'. Man, who unprecedented and even increasing quest for better quality of life and materialistic comforts' and a state, which claims sovereignty over its natural resources, in its zeal to develop, have been excessively exploiting and indiscriminately consuming natural resources at their command.

The excessive exploitation of natural resources and their imprudent use rather, misuse, have unfortunately led to a serious ecological crisis. The United Nations Economic and Social Commission for Asia and the Pacific (ESCAP) warned early in February 1985, that the Asian Environment, already in a critical state, is likely to burden with additional load resulting from development activities. Considering technology in the perspective of environment, we faced with lack of environmentally friendly technology. We need is to search and increase the environmentally friendly technology and at the same time stopping or at least reducing the use of those technology which affects the environment adversely.

2.3.3 AGRICULTURAL DEVELOPMENT:

Agricultural Development means expansion of agricultural land and increase in agricultural production. It is due to development of modem scientific techniques, advanced technologies, increased production and use of chemical fertilizers, expansion in irrigation facilities and development of high-yielding varieties of seeds, etc. This has solved the problem of growing demand of food due to increase in world's population on one hand; it has also created or is creating hazardous environmental problems of serious concern of the other hand. Thus, modem economic and technological man is at the cross road of dangers in all directions. The agricultural development degrades the environment in a variety of ways, e.g. (i) through indiscriminate application of chemical fertilizers and pesticides and insecticides, (ii) through the increase in irrational faculties and amount of irrigation, and (iii) by making changes in biological communities etc.

The forestlands have converted into agricultural lands, the productivity increases through intensive cultivation by use of machines and modem scientific techniques, application of chemical fertilizers, pesticides, insecticides and herbicides, increase in the frequency and area 0f watering of agricultural fields, etc. All these processes and measures in causes several serious problems arising out of agricultural development is the increase 0f human population at alarming rate. Therefore, the foremost steps required to take up is to **stop population growth.**

2.3.4 POPULATION GROWTH:

Today the growth of human population is more significant in lowering the environmental quality and ecological balance.

For example, industrial expansion, urban growth, agricultural development, increase in means of transport and communication, etc. are the results of population growth.

The development of scientific techniques and advanced technologies are in order to save the humanity from hunger, and natural calamity and disaster. Thus, it is obvious that overpopulation and poverty are the root causes of environmental degradation and ecological imbalance. The increase in population led to more exploitation of natural resources, which means environmental problems. The problem of population growth has become a global phenomenon, which got its alarming proportion in India. India is the second largest populated country in the world of human race against the 2.4 percent of global land.

The increase in the rate of population growth puts a heavy demand on the natural resources like water, air, soil etc. According to a study, the tropical forest is shrinking by million hectares a year. Topsoil is being lost at the rate of 26 billion tons a year.

The problem of deforestation also has its alarming proportion all over the world. The problem of population having very personal nature has long been a very emotional issue. However, there is a direct relationship between increase in population numbers and environmental impact. More people require more food, more land for buildings, more minerals, more water and more energy. The side effects include enhanced of chemicals, chemical fertilizers, insecticides, pesticides, deforestation, increased population and heavy load on transport.

Due to the rapid growth of population, the world is steadily becoming urban. In 1950, 29.3 percent of the global population lived in urban areas but by mid 1990, the share of the urban population increased to 43 percent (2 billion). India is no exception to the problem of urbanization. The growth rate of mega cities is changing. The problem of fast emergence of mega cities is putting undue pressure on the necessities.

Based on a global average it has been calculated roughly that a city of one million inhabitants consumes every about 625,000 metric tons of water, 2000 metric tons of food and 9500 metric tons of fuel. Further, the inhabitants of mega cities also face the problem of air and noise pollution due to the rise in the number of personal vehicles and other means of transportation. According to one study in Delhi, emission from automobile amounts to 65% of the total air pollution. Another study states, Delhi is acquiring the dubious distinction of becoming one of the noisiest cities in the world with the growing number of vehicles. In some places, levels of noise are higher than the permissible limit of noise, which is 50 decibels in the night. Thus, the population growth has become the main cause of environmental pollution, which needs to be reduced through some comprehensive legislation.

2.3.5 INDUSTRIAL DEVELOPMENT:

The rapid Industrial Development/ growth give economic prosperity to human society. It gives a new dimension to the socio-economic structure, a material comfort to the people and creates environmental problems in many folds. In fact, the glittering effects of industrialization have affected. In the minds of the public, that industrialization considered as the parameter of modernity and as a necessary element of "socio-economic development" of nation. Rapid rate of industrialization resulted into rapid rate of exploitation of natural resources and increased industrial output.

E.g., Exploitation of natural resources and industrial production have created several lethal environmental problems and caused large-scale environmental problems and ecological imbalance at global, regional and local level in a variety of ways.

Exploitation of natural resources to meet the industrial demand of raw materials are: (I) the reduction of forest covers, (ii) Excavation of land for mining purposes, (iii) reduction in arable land due to industrial expansion, (iv) lowering of groundwater level due to excessive withdrawal of groundwater, (v) collapsing of ground surface due to withdrawal of mineral oil and groundwater etc. Besides desired production, there are numerous undesired outputs from the factories such as industrial wastes, polluted water, toxic gases, chemical precipitates, aerosol etc., which pollute air, water, land, soils and thus degrade the environment. The industrialized countries have increased the concentration of pollutants emitted from the factories in to the air; water and land to such an extent that they have degraded the environment to the critical limit and have brought the human society on the brink of its destruction.

The adverse effects of industrialization may change the overall character of natural system and the chain effects sometimes become suicidal for human society. Majority of the impacts of industrialization related to pollution and environmental degradation. The release of toxic elements into the environment through the application of chemical fertilizers, pesticides and insecticides (output of chemical industries) changes the food chain, food web and physical and chemical properties of soils. The release of industrial wastes into ponds, tanks, and lakes, rivers and seas, the water is contaminated and causes several diseases and deaths of organisms and thus disturbs ecological balance of aquatic ecosystem. Increasing industrial expansion leads to release of enormous quantities of pollutants (ions of chlorine, sulfur, bicarbonate, nitrate, sodium, magnesium, phosphate) through sewage effluents into the rivers, the lakes, and thus contaminating the water.

Release of several gases, smokes, ashes, and other aerosols from the chimneys of the factories adversely affects the environment in number of ways. The burning of hydrocarbon fuels (coal and petroleum) has increased the concentration of CO_2 in the atmosphere and thus has changed the natural gaseous composition of the atmosphere. The increase in concentration of CO_2 in the atmosphere change global radiation. There by increasing the level of sensible heat in the atmosphere because of CO_2, that intensifies the greenhouse effects of the atmosphere as CO_2 allows the solar radiation to pass through the atmosphere.

The release of 'chlorofluorocarbons' in the atmosphere causes **depletion of ozone layer**. Ozone is a tri- atomic molecule consisting of three atoms of Oxygen. It exists in gaseous form in the stratosphere and is unstable compared to the diatomic Oxygen molecule. **Ozone** forms a protective covering in the atmosphere, filters the harmful ultraviolet rays, and prevents them from reaching earth's surface.

2.3.5.1 DEPLETION OF OZONE: Depletion of Ozone layer means less absorption of ultraviolet solar rays and thus substantial increase in the temperature at the earth surface. Depletion of ozone may cause change in weather and climatic conditions at global and regional levels. Severe damages to plant and animal lives and thus may cause ecological imbalance. It may cause dangerous diseases "like skin cancer" etc.

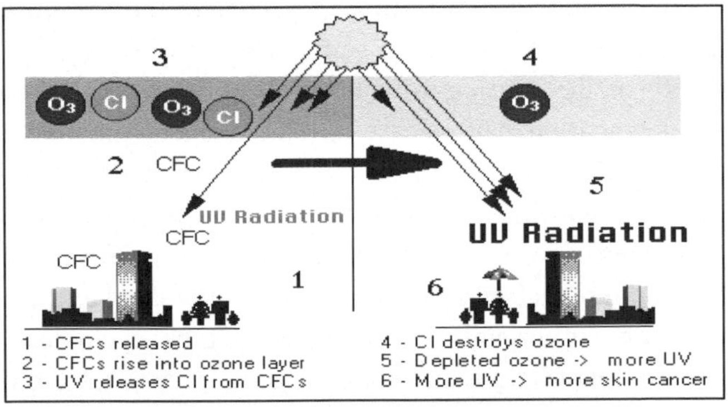

Fig.12: Showing the Difference between Atmosphere with and without Ozone

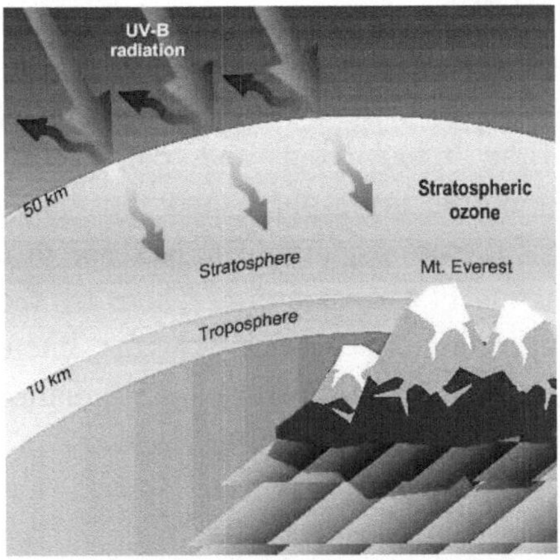

Fig.13; Showing Entry of U.V. Radiation from Sun to Earth

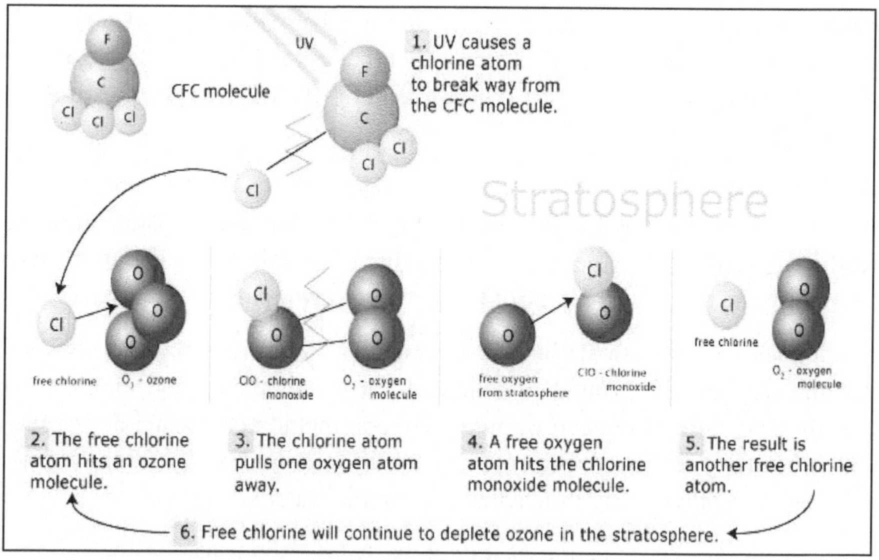

Fig. 14: Effect of U.V. Radiation on Atmosphere

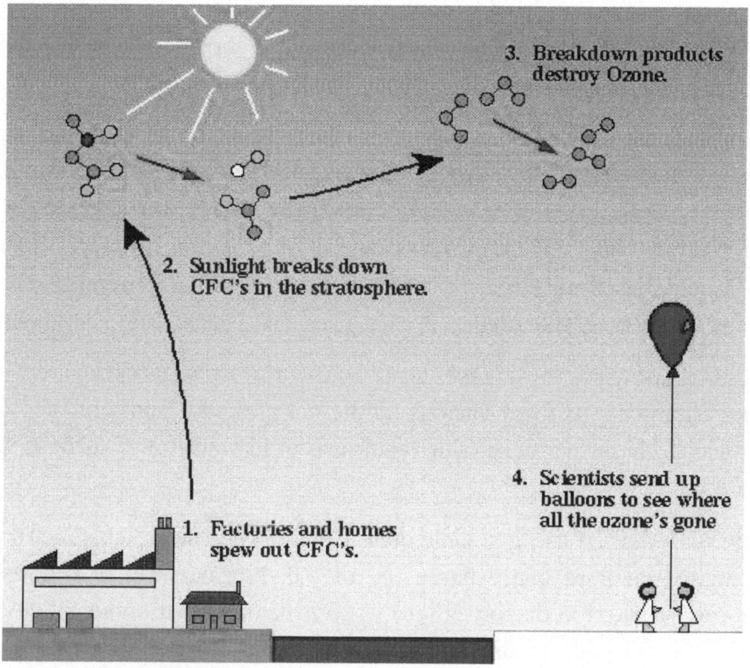

Fig. 15: Effect of Industries Pollution on Atmosphere

Release of toxic gases through advertent and in advertent actions of man causes environmental hazards, which destroy all types of life forms in the affected areas. The Bhopal Gas Tragedy (December3-4, 1984, India) is an example of disastrous effects of modern industrialization.

2.3.5.2 ACID RAINS: Urban smog, nuclear holocaust, etc., are the other forms of environmental hazards emanating from industries. "Acid rain" is a broad term used to describe several ways that acids fall out of the atmosphere. A more precise term is acid deposition, which has two parts: wet and dry.

Wet deposition refers to acidic rain, fog, and snow. As this acidic water flows over and through the ground, it affects a variety of plants and animals. The strength of the effects depend on many factors, including how acidic the water is, the chemistry and buffering capacity of the soils involved, and the types of fish, trees, and other living things that rely on the water.

Dry deposition refers to acidic gases and particles. About half of the acidity in the atmosphere falls back to earth through dry deposition. The wind blows these acidic particles and gases onto buildings, cars, homes, and trees. Dry deposited gases and particles can also be washed from trees and other surfaces by rain storms. When that happens, the runoff water adds those acids to the acid rain, making the combination more acidic than the falling rain alone.

Prevailing winds blow the compounds that cause both wet and dry acid deposition across state and national borders, and sometimes over hundreds of miles. Scientists discovered, and have confirmed, that sulfur dioxide (SO_2) and nitrogen oxides (NO_x) are the primary causes of acid rain. In the US, about 2/3 of all SO_2 and 1/4 of all NO_x comes from electric power generation that relies on burning fossil fuels like coal.

Acid rain occurs when these gases react in the atmosphere with water, oxygen, and other chemicals to form various acidic compounds. Sunlight increases the rate of most of these reactions. The result is a mild solution of sulfuric acid and nitric acid.

Acid rain is measured using a scale called "pH." The lower substance's pH, the more acidic it is. Pure water has a pH of 7.0. Normal rain is slightly acidic because carbon dioxide dissolves into it, so it has a pH of about 5.5. As of the year 2000, the most acidic rain falling in the US has a pH of about 4.3.

Its effects are: Acid rain causes acidification of lakes and streams and contributes to damage of trees at high elevations (for example, red spruce trees above 2,000 feet) and many sensitive forest soils. In addition, acid rain accelerates the decay of building materials and paints, including irreplaceable buildings, statues, and sculptures that are part of our nation's cultural heritage. Prior to falling to the earth, SO_2 and NO_x gases and their particulate matter derivatives, sulfates and nitrates, contribute to visibility degradation and harm public health.

Because nitrogen oxides are created in the process of burning coal and other fossil fuels, some power plants are changing the way they burn coal. A great way to reduce acid rain is to produce energy without using fossil fuels.

The original acid (hydrogen ions) has been converted to water in these reactions. Limestone Neutralization: When acid rain falls to the earth, it undergoes a new round of physical and chemical changes. Alkaline or basic soils, such as those rich in limestone, calcium carbonate, can neutralize the acid directly.

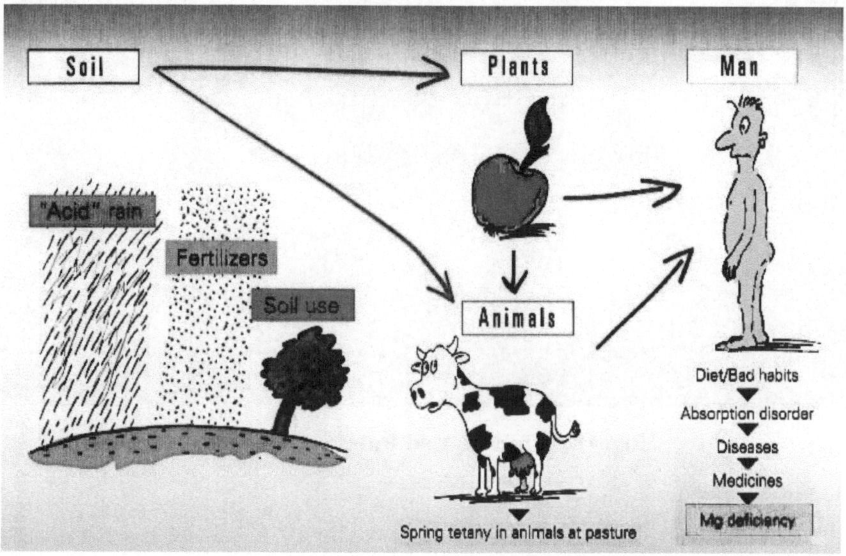

Fig. 16: Effects of acid rains on human beings

Fig.17: Effect of Acid Rains on Animals

Fig. 18: Effect of Acid Rains on Humans

Today India has become the 10th largest industrial nation of the World. However, at the same time it is one of the most polluted countries of the world as far as “industrial pollution" and “hazardous wastes” are concerned. The real problem that faced by us is from the unregulated industrial development. The largest volume of wastes discharged is in form of liquid effluents. The industrial effluents that discharged in to the aquatic environment through different ways contain different pollutants different sources. Typical floating materials are oils and gases released from petrochemical and automobile plants. The tanning processes, paper, and pulp manufacturing discharge coloring wastes into fresh water. These materials make water unsightly, block sunlight, interfere re aeration process hence affect the physical properties of the waters.

The industrial effluents may contain suspended matters. These matters may be organic or inorganic. The former have the same effect on the physical properties of the receiving waters. The organic suspended matters decompose the dissolved oxygen content and consequently reduce the oxygen quantity. The decomposition process produces noxious gases and odors. Chemical substances present in the Industrial wastes cause physical and chemical pollution of the watercourses.

Acids and alkalis discharged from different industrial units disturb the physical composition of water by raising the acidity or alkalinity. Soluble salts of heavy metals such as lead, mercury, cadmium, zinc copper, nickel, arsenic released in sufficient quantity are highly toxic and hazardous. Industry is central to our socio-economic development. The socio economic development of human society made possible through goods and services provided by industries.

However, industries extract raw materials from "Nature" and discharge "Products" from their front doors and "Pollution" from their back doors to the environment. Therefore, necessary attention needs to focus not only on the increase in the quantum of production but also on the environmental deterioration because of industrialization.

2.3.6 URBANIZATION:

Migrating people from rural areas to urban areas for their employment and improving economic growth results in expansion of new urban areas and industrial expansion are responsible for rapid rate of exploitation of natural resources, which tends to environmental degradation and pollution in the developed and developing countries.

The level of urbanization in the developed countries of the world has already reached its peak. The accumulation of wealth and availability of economic and job opportunity in the urban centers have resulted into the concentration of population in the congested metropolitan areas leads formation and growth of big slum areas.

In fact, increasing urbanization means increase in concentration of human population in limited space, which result in the increase of buildings, roads and streets, sewage and storm drains, vehicles (motorcars, trucks, buses, motor cycles, etc.). For example, increasing population of the urban centers uses enormous amount of water for various purposes. The sewage water, if untreated, pollutes the streams and lakes.

Urban centers when combined with industrial sectors become more hazardous from the standpoint of environmental problems and pollution. Huge quantity of aerosols and gases emitted from Chimneys of factories and vehicles, which form "**DUST DOME**" over the cities. These **DUST DOMES** cause **'POLLUTION DOMES'** over the cities. The urban and industrial growth has resulted into rapid rate of deterioration of the quantity of air that emitted from the vehicles, factories and household appliances. Vehicles contribute about 60 percent of the pollution of Indian capital city of Delhi. Calcutta and Bombay metropolitan areas have also reached high level of air pollution. According to the survey report of the National Environmental Research Institute, Nagpur (India) the level of air pollution in Delhi, Calcutta, Bombay, Madras, Ahmadabad, Cochin, Hyderabad, Kanpur, Nagpur etc. has gone up.

2.3.6.1 UNPLANNED URBANIZATION

The skewed urban development has deteriorated the environment considerably. The urban areas suffer from their own plight, squatter settlements, lack of sanitation and water supply, overcrowding and pollution. The cities in India are facing environmental problems like lack of sanitation, chronic shortage of traffic congestion etc. Moreover, the domestic and industrial waste disposal in the urban areas is very serious. Most of the cities are lacking sewer systems. For example, studies by the Central Board for the prevention and control of water pollution have shown that the discharge of community wastage and industrial effluents is the major cause of water pollution. At present 56% of Class-I cities and 87% of Class II towns do not possess sewerage facilities. We therefore need a well-controlled and well-managed process of urbanization to curb rural urban migration and other related problems.

2.3.7 MODERN PRODUCTIVE TECHNOLOGY:

The development of modern technologies has definitely created most of the present day environmental problems. Environmental crisis is thus the inevitable result of a counter ecological pattern of productive growth. The environmental problems are held to be associated with productive processes concerning on synthetic and non-biodegradable materials. Modern techniques have enabled the man construct huge dams and reservoirs for the purpose of irrigation and generation of hydroelectricity, which is immensely required by the industrial sector to augment the production processes and by the domestic sector to increase the comfort of human beings.

Such activities create several environmental problems of greater dimension. Large reservoirs submerge vast areas of natural forests and thus degrade the environment in the source catchments area of the concerned river. Leakage of toxic gases from chemical plants not only pollute the air but also causes deaths of human beings, plants and animals and causes impairment of human bodies for several years even for few generations.

The Bhopal Gas Tragedy of December 1984 is the fittest example of lethal effects of the failures of modem technology. Numerous toxic industrial wastes also cause serious environmental problems. The most dangerous aspect of modem technologies is the production of a host of toxic chemicals, synthetic materials and biologically non-degradable materials. The most dangerous aspect of modern technologies is the problem of disposal of nuclear waste materials coming out of the nuclear reactor plants.

2.3.8 THERMAL POWER PLANTS (COAL BURNT):

Power Plants in public or private sector mainly use coal for generation of electricity. About 62% of the coal produced in our country utilized for generation of electricity, which accounts of 65% of power generation. This process results in the accumulation of various by¬products such as bottom ash, boiler slag and fly ash. Fly ash alone amounts to more than 70% of the total quantity. Disposal of these huge amounts of fly ash is a difficult and sensitive task. However, this material used in manufacture of cement, brick and used as soil conditioner but these activities have not gained much popularity due to economical and social consideration. Even if the fly ash utilized for the above-mentioned activities, it will not be possible to utilize even 30% to 40% of the ash produced. Thus, there is a need to store the ash produced in such a way as to have minimum damage to air, water and soil bodies.

A super thermal power plant built on about 800 acres of land normally requires 1200 acres for ash disposal. Because of the ash production trends, the area requirement for dumping of the ash is around 4000hectares.

Power plants are preferably away from the human settlements and more over on wastelands, but with course of time some of the cultivable area covered for ash mount site. Presence of ash particularly in the atmosphere is of major concern to the people living close to the plant site. This is particularly severe in summers due to prevailing high wind speeds. The finer fractions of fly ash are potentially harmful as they deposited in lungs/pulmonary tissues of respiratory track when inhaled.

2.3.9 POVERTY:

Indira Gandhi had stated in the Stockholm conference in 1972, that **"Poverty was the greatest polluter".** The people exploit excessively the natural resources of the country for meeting their basic needs like food, fuel, shelter, employment and fodder for their cattle. Poverty and need indeed the greatest polluter and there by necessary steps should be required to bring the poor people above the poverty line.

It's the poor who depend most on natural resources for their livelihoods, and who suffer most from the impacts of climate change, deforestation, overfishing and other environmental problems. Environment and development issues can't be separated.

Universal access to basic education and vocational training, community information on sound agricultural methods, waste management, natural resources management, coastal protection, water resources management, fisheries management are all essential in reducing poverty as well as in reducing the effects of poverty on the environment. Measures to stop deforestation and re-forestation programs can secure a more sustainable resource base that benefits the poor. Local low-cost production of fuel-efficient stoves and heating devices can go a long way in reducing the energy bill of low-income households while protecting the environment.

On 25th September 2015, 193 countries of the United Nations General Assembly adopted the 2030 agenda for Sustainable Development which contains 17 Sustainable Development Goals (SDGs).

The first and the foremost Sustainable Development goal are to "End Poverty in all forms everywhere". Each and every country of the world is looking forward to eradicate poverty so that even the poor and vulnerable people also enjoy equal rights to economic resources, healthy living conditions as well as access to basic infrastructure and technology. Moreover, there should not be any doubt that poor nations and poor people are more severely vulnerable to effects of environmental damage than the rich. Over the past few decades, average living standards have risen and the gap between the very rich and the very poor has broadened. But the question here arises "Why is poverty still prevailing in the world?

There can be many reasons but, two biggest factors contributing to poverty are: Lack of education and improper implementation of poverty eradication policies at the grass-root level. Often, many international reports claim that poverty contributes to environmental degradation. Due to lack of sufficient resources and improper knowledge poverty stricken people tend to overuse every resource available to them when their survival is at stake. But generally, it tends to forget that poor people are the most undefended ones when it comes to effects of environmental pollution, climate change and global warming.

It is very important for everyone to recognize that poverty and environmental issues are interrelated. Poverty among people puts stress on the environment whereas environmental problems cause severe suffering to the poor. People, whether they be rich or poor, consume water, food, and natural resources in order to remain alive. All economic activities are directly, indirectly or remotely based on natural resources and any pressure on natural resources can cause environmental stress. Environmental damage can prevent people, especially the poor, from having good and hygienic living standards. As poor people rely more directly on the environment than the rich for their survival, they are mostly on the receiving end of environmental problems

Poverty often causes people to put relatively more pressure on the environment which results in larger families (due to high death rates and insecurity), improper human waste disposal leading to unhealthy living conditions, more pressure on fragile land to meet their needs, overexploitation of natural resources and more deforestation. Insufficient knowledge about agricultural practices can also lead to decline in crop yield and productivity etc.

On the other hand, environmental problems add more to the miseries of poor people. Environmental problems cause more suffering among them as environmental damage increases the impact of floods and other environmental catastrophes. Soil erosion, land degradation and deforestation lead to decline in food production along with shortage of wood for fuel contributes to inflation. In short, the worst consequences of environmental deterioration, whether they be economical, social, or related to metal or physical wellbeing, are experienced by the poor people.

More rigorous efforts should be undertaken by the governments of all countries to eradicate poverty and in turn, to save deprived people from the dreadful implications of environmental damage. There should be more collaborative partnerships among all sections of the society so that even the people living in poverty are linked to the world through their participation in social, political, and economical spheres along with their active participation in environmental regeneration.

One should strongly believe that there cannot be any environmental solution without alleviating poverty from the world."

****

Chapter – 3

ENVIRONMENT AND ANCIENT INDIA

3.1. Environment and Ancient India, 3.2 Environmental Ethics and Ancient India, 3.3 Environment Protection with Religion.

3.1 ENVIRONMENT AND ANCIENT INDIA:

In ancient India, man's life was assumed to be of 100 years and it was sub-divided into four stages, each stage comprising of 25years i.e. **Brahmacharya** (Celibacy), **Gruhastya** (Householder), **Vanaprastha** (Gradual detachment) and **Sanyasa** (Renunciation of the world).

In those days, there were no schools, colleges or universities and hence learned men and scholars who were hailed as Acharyas and Gurus imparted education. The Guru was a father, a guardian and an advisor. In this connection, it was mandatory for a young male to spend number of years in 'Guru Kula'. This was some kind of a residential college.

The students lived with the guru's family members, each performing a specific set of chores, apart from imbibing education and ideology. These gurukulas or ashrams were located far away from cities towns and villages. Since they lived in a natural environment, the students as well as their gurus were concerned about its preservation. They protected trees and worshipped them as **Vriksha Devta** (Tree God), the forest covers as **Van Devta** (Forest God) and the rivers as sources of water for delicious life. The ancient people cared for wildlife too. Terms and titles such as **Nag Devta** (Snake God), **Kamdhenu** (the cow that fulfills desires) and **Kalpavriksha** (the wish –fulfilling tree) symbolized the benefits that accrued to human beings from nature and their respect for wildlife. Thus, pantheism or animism, by whatever name that call it, eventually pointed to ecological balance and conservation of nature.

In the primitive ages of human civilization, the man was in the state of nature. The man was roaming up and down in the forests, without speech, without any industry and without home. The man depends on the nature in its absolute terms.

To the man, in the state of nature, the first feeling was that of hunger and self-preservation. Modem psychologists also regard hunger and sex as a prim instinct. Hunger was the first concern of the primitive man. Self-preservation cut across its bounds into self-aggrandizement. The growth of culture and civilization must be made from perspective of the fullness of reality. In the fullness of reality, there is nature at large and the man enlarging his self at the expense of nature.

In every moment of his life, man was imbibing the resources of nature without yielding anything in return to the nature. The breath he inhaled and exhaled, the water he drink and the food he eat and excrete in were all the things in respect of which he was the drone of nature and each man had to do it.

For living and enjoying life, man used the nature, but unfortunately, the same had abused. In this process water, food, land and air had used indiscriminately. During this Man adversely affected, his health, his comfort, his aesthetic sense, his efficiency and his capacity to attain a satisfactory social adjustment. Man use air, water, Land and food for his life affected the dynamics of plant and animal life on earth by altering ecological balances. It is to state that the balance in ecology is the same thing as equilibrium in nature. Equilibrium in nature is the cosmic justice and the force that sustains this equilibrium is cosmic law or the law of nature. It is cosmic law, which upholds cosmic justice, which is justice in nature exhibited in the ordinary principle of cosmic harmony or proportion of nature.

Pollution is innate urge in the cosmic cause. Releasing energy for creation is cosmic inheritance of the creature. Adam in the Genesis of the Holy Bible is the testimony of the creative urge, which explains the creation is the first cause of pollution with regard to any creature, and with reference to ecology.

The advent of the Homespun is the point that nature was having culminated and its evolutionary process leaving the negative and animal life multiply of its own accord. This culminating stage of the evolutionary process was itself representative of the measure of ecological balance coveted by nature. Since arrival of the meditative life of the Homespun, therefore, the biological evolution has come to a standstill and evolutionary process has thereafter rested upon re-production of biological life both on the botanical and on the zoological levels. The evolution of meditative life aspires for attainment of values to human life. The meditative evolution is a process of regeneration of values. On the meditative phase, the evolution of life implies merely the evolution of self.

3.2 ENVIRONMENTAL ETHICS AND ANCIENT INDIA:

India has a long tradition of protecting and worshipping the nature. The land, trees and even animals placed on a high pedestal since Vedic times. Since time immemorial, Indians had believed that the life depends on nature. The activities of customary Indian from morning to evening governed according to the movements and various positions of the sun and the moon. Even our houses and buildings built according to **'Vastu'** considering the direction of the wind and the sun. All the systems of our life organized in such a manner that water conserved and its purity a kept in view. Plants and forests developed in such a manner that the natural environment is preserved and protected.

According to ancient Indian mythology, the God prevail the whole universe. This point of view has helped Indian to maintain a constant link with nature. The concept of divine world is based on the principle that God creates divine forces to run the universe. The powers of God in different worlds are in the form of different entities and are governed the universe in accordance with the principle of Lela or God's Play.

The Aryas worshipped Nature. They were fascinated by their natural surroundings. Gods representing the forces of nature are mentioned in the hymns of Rig Veda. Rta was the term used to mean the natural law of the cosmic order and morality. It was the regulator of the whole Universe. Dyaus, sky, Prithvi, earth, Varuna, the sky god and protector of Rta and Indra, Savitri, Mitra and Pushan represented different powers of the Sun such as heat, light and nourishment. Vishnu was the symbol of swift movement while Rudra and Maruts were the gods of storm and winds. Shiva was the later name given to Rudra. Vayu and Vata were other gods of winds while Parjanya was the god of rain. There were gods on earth also. Agni was an important deity. Soma was regarded as essential for sacrifice. Saraswati as river goddess on earth. However, the most loved goddess was Usha (Dawn) belonging to both earth and heaven.

The messages of environmental conservation contained in the Vedic and Puranic literatures, in the Upanishads, Arthashastra, Charak Samhita, Ramayana and Mahabharata are all based on Hindu religious philosophy. "Non-violence" that is, non-injury to both the living as well the non-living creations of nature such as plants, animals, air, water, land (earth), hill and forest is the core of Hindu religious philosophy which extended up to Jainism and Buddhism. Traditional Hindus believe that trees can bring peace, prosperity and consolation to humankind. The primitive Hindu societies of India represented by the tribals (aborigines) living in mountains and forests have significantly contributed a protection and preservation of several virgin forest patches in rich in biodiversity. They are called "sacred groves" (Forest of God) and are left untouched by the local people. Rig-Veda has dwelt upon various components of the ecosystem and their importance.

According to **Rig-Veda**, all life on this planet evolved from apah (water). Water is usually acknowledged as the basic need of all living creatures upon the face of this earth. There are copious references in Vedic literature about medicinal properties of water, uses of water, last but not the least the importance of conservation and preservation of water. Pure water is termed as **'divya-jal'** due to its following properties: Sheetam (cold to touch), Suchihi (clean), Shivam (replete with useful minerals and trace of useful elements), Istham (transparent), and Vimalam Lahu Shadgunam (its acid-base balance should not exceed normal limits).

Rig-Veda says "**Thousands and Hundreds of years if you want to enjoy the fruits and happiness of life then take up systematic planting of trees.**"

In ancient days all the objects of the universe recognized that the divine being present in the Panchabhutas (the five elements) viz., air, water, fire, earth and Ether. Our ancestors have perceived divine existence in trees, medicines, rivers, lakes, mountains and all living beings and all creatures. Due to such extraordinary awareness regarding the nature and ecological balance, India was the most advanced country of the world. It has considered that a part of our traditions and cultural values not only to protect the environment but also to maintain the ecological balance.

The ancient Indian custom of storing drinking water was in brass vessels for good health that proved now scientifically by researchers. Microbiologists affirm that water stored in brass containers that help combat many water-borne diseases and therefore used in developing countries rather than their cheaper counterpart's i. e plastic containers.

The scientific principle involved in this is the fact that any metal or alloy tends to disrupt biological systems. The element acts by interfering with the membranes and enzymes of cells; for bacteria, this can mean death. Pots made of brass, (an alloy of copper and zinc), shed copper particles into the water that they contain. However, the miniscule amount that circulates into the water, while destroying the bacteria cannot harm human beings.

In ancient Indian way of life, people before stepping foot on the earth from bed in the morning, people addressed the earth as mother and requested the mother earth's forgiveness for stepping .Hindus respect the rivers as tirtha (places of pilgrimage) and worship Gods abode is considered in lakes and mountains from which rivers originate.

The concept of Panchavati is the conclusive proof of the importance, which had given to the Forest in Ancient India. The word Panchavati found in the vocabulary of all Indian languages that confirms that the tradition to protect forest pervading the whole country since primitive ages.

The term Panchavati consists of two words viz., Panch and Vati. Panch means five and vati means grove, therefore, 'Panchavati' means a grove has five trees. Panchavati also means a forest in which there are five kinds of trees. It conveys a sense of totality of plurality.

The most important classification of forests in ancient Indian literature based on the form of the forest and the purpose it served. Brundavans (forests) classified into three categories viz., Mahavana, Tapovana and Srivana. Mahavana was impenetrable and was a place for mystical manifestation of natural and supernatural forces. Tapovana was not impenetrable like Mahavana and one could enter in this category of forest. The Mahavan and Tapovan too had abounded in flora, plants and trees. Sadhus, Sanyasis and Rishies attached to this kind of forests due to its easy accessibility and serenity. In these types of forests, the Rishis retreated to their ashrams to study and apply the fruits of their studies into practicalities, had ample time also for meditation and for religious practices. They could become the famous Acharyas who imparted theoretical, practical, and spiritual knowledge. Most of the festivals of the Indian villages used to celebrate in Srivana. The Panchayats of the villages also held here.

Therefore, it had stated that the higher values of life in the ancient India interconnected with Vanaprastha. It can be inferred from the Ashrams (the law relating to the various stages of human life) namely, Brahamacharyashram, Gruhasthashram, Vanaprasthashram and Sanyasa-ashram. Out of these four Ashrams, the activities get last two Ashrams i.e., Vanaprastha and Sanyasashrama completely carried in the forests as they make integral part of life. Even in the Gruhastha and Vanprastha-ashramas, the life on an ancient Indian era was infinitely connected and dependent on the forests. Therefore, from the foregoing discussion, it is evident that the people of India had a very close relationship with plants and trees. The forests have a profound contribution in the diurnal life of a human being. Hence, plants and trees treated as a part of one's family.

Conclusion:

Ancient civilizations respected nature, as reflected both by their lifestyles and by the complex web of mythology and legends that have been passed down to us from those days. This love for nature coexisted with a deep reverence for God. At regular intervals in history, societies grew more complex, and less intimate with nature. Yet each time that humankind forgot the power of nature, it was only divine intervention that prevented certain apocalypse.

Today's society, unfortunately, is neither nature loving nor God-fearing. Everyone worships only material wealth and think nothing of exploiting our natural surroundings to increase their wealth. This stands on the verge of another great cataclysm, but it is unlikely that God will intervene this time to rescue a people who have forgotten him and discarded traditions so completely.

It is the need of the hour that to look back into our past and adopt the rich traditions shall enable to live in harmony with nature. One must rediscover our roots, value morality and strength of character more than to value money and must strive to follow the ancients' path of virtue and righteousness, which will lead to God.

Dr. Abdul Kalam's words: "Ancient India was a knowledge society that contributed a great deal to civilization. We need to recover the status and become a knowledge power. Spirituality must be integrated with education. We should ignite our dormant inner energy and let it guide our lives. The radiance of such minds embarked on constructive endeavor will bring peace, prosperity, and bliss to the nation".

3.3 ENVIRONMENT PROTECTION WITH RELIGION:

Religion commonly pertains to the spiritual domain while the science and technology are viewed as systems pertaining to the material domain. Issue of material development and progress has, therefore, bell left to the charge of scientific experts while religious belief has left to guide the inner spiritual development of the individuals. The ecological crisis in the ultimate analysis can lead to the undermining of material existence. The paradoxical situation in which rapid scientific and technological change has been associated with rapid destruction of the material basis of life, poses the most critical challenges of our times.

This challenge creates two situations. On one hand, it allows the reappraisal of religious and cultural beliefs as social systems for ordering the material and secular world. On the other hand, it allows the pre-appraisal of scientific beliefs in terms of their adequacy in knowing nature's patterns, rhythms and relationship in order to maintain them ecologically.

It is obvious that Indian and cultural traditions are very rich in values. These include all the major religions. Religious traditions and beliefs in India played a vital role in protection of environment. The earliest religious thought of India is 'Rig-Veda', which itself begin with a vivid description of five elements i.e., Earth, Air, Water, Energy and Ether constitute our universe and give the life support for man, animal and the base for all inns of human activity and vegetation.

The Indian saints, sages and seers (Rishi's) of ancient times were great visionaries who perceived the creation of universe in a scientific manner and revealed the mysteries of cosmic evolution with profound wisdom and theories, perhaps too advanced at that time for the world to understand. It is only now that with the modern concepts like quantum mechanics and string theory through the efforts of physicists and nuclear scientists, the ancient theories revealed in the Upanishads are being revisited.

The ancient scriptures also present in great detail, inter alia, the evolution of earth, the science of rainfall, its measurement and forecast, climatology, meteorology, hydrology, water use and management, environmental protection, agricultural planning etc. while describing and hailing the five basic elements of Nature. Even today water festivals, popularly called `Kumbh' are held every twelfth year on astronomically specific occasions at four places in India where an estimated 10-30 million people congregate on the banks of holy rivers for a dip. Water festivals throughout the country also celebrated on auspicious days. From birth until death in an Indian society, water remains an essential ingredient in performing all rituals.

In fact, the concern for environment protection has traced in the period between 321 and 300 BC itself. The ancient Indian law on environment protection has found in **"Kautilya's Arthashatra".** It was the dharma of everyone in the society to protect the nature. The people worshipped the objects of nature. The trees, water, land gained important position in the ancient times. The cultural and religious heritage of Indian shows a deep concern for the protection and preservation of the environment. All religions regulated the conduct of humankind in such a manner, which was conducive to nature and not adverse to nature.

The yajna or sacrifice fire, apparently done to worship one or the other deity that helps in purifying the air and thus keeping the environment healthy. In **Yajurveda**, the significance of yajna has explained by stating that "ghee" and "firewood" offered into the sacrificial fire, it dissolves them to their subtlety to settle in the atmosphere and thus making it free from impurities and stink.

Samaveda highlights the importance of sacrificial fire, as it helps in keeping away mosquito's and other insects. Yajna or sacrificial fire is also considered the cause of biological evolution.

Shloka 14, chapter 3 of **Shri Bhagwat Gita** explains that the blood and the semen is chemical transformation of the cereal consumed. From the seminal sperm, creatures are begotten. However, the cereal grows because of water that rains and the rains bought about through the yajna or the sacrificial fires.

The Hindu Declaration on Climate Change, presented in December 2009 at the Parliament of the World's Religions in Australia, clearly expresses the state of affairs: "Our beloved Earth, so touchingly looked upon as the Universal Mother, has nurtured mankind through millions of years of growth and evolution. Now centuries of rapacious exploitation of the planet have caught up with us, and a radical change in our relationship with nature is no longer an option. It is a matter of survival. One cannot continue to destroy nature without also destroying ourselves." How far one has drifted from the reverential sentiment expressed in "My salutations to you, "O" Bhudevi, consort of the all-pervasive Lord, forgive me for placing my feet upon you."

Pope Paul VI, in his message to the United Nations conference on the human environment held at Stockholm in June 1972 stated that the environment and resources are for everyone, they are inalienable property of everyone that there does not exist over this universal property discretionary sovereignty exempting from responsibility towards the humanity of today and tomorrow. This message of Pope Paul makes it amply clear that there is a close link between Christianity and environment and the thrust is for sustainable development.

Jainism is also based on the principle, which is in close harmony with nature and help in protecting and preserving the nature.

The **holy Quran** declares that everything is created from water. Thus, there is a significance of benefit purity of water. **Allah** is considered the owner of land and humankind is the trustee or guardian whereas other living creatures are considered the beneficiaries. In Islam, also there is close harmony between man and nature.

All major religions view that man is only among many creatures to enjoy nature's beauties and bounties. Nature has given to him in trust to make wise and responsible use of it. NO religion justifies the destructive attitude of modem man, which has developed toward his environment. Indifferent languages and with different symbols, all religions treat nature as a God given gift, some even stating, **"God is Omnipresent in the manifestations of nature".**

****

Chapter - 4

HINDU MYTHOLOGY

4.1. Hindu mythology on environment protection, 4.2 Hinduism: The Origin of the Universe, 4.3 Origin of Environmental Science from Vedas, 4.4. The Teachings of Atharva Veda, 4.5 Trees Associated With The Gods And Goddesses, 4.6 Charka Samhita, 4.7 Manu (Manusmriti), 4.8 Animals Associated with God / Goddess , 4.9 Teachings of Yajurveda, 4.10 Bishnoi's Faith and Environment Protection, 4.11.Hinduism and Ecology.

4.1 HINDU MYTHOLOGY ON ENVIRONMENT PROTECTION:

Hindu religion is one of the oldest religions of the world. Ever since Vedic times, the main motto of social life was to have in harmony with the nature. Sages, saints and the great philosophers of India were lived in forests and on mountains for meditation and taught Vedas, Upanishad and Smithies. It was perched that in one form or other worshipful attitudes were towards the earth, sky, air, water, trees, plants and animals to keep benevolent attitudes. It regarded as scared duty of the humankind. The Hindu religion and law enshrined the respect for nature, environmental harmony and conservation. It instanced man to show reverence for the presence of divinity in nature.

God has sent man in to this life so circumstanced with hunger and desire that he must work. Without work human civilization would be a jungle of disease, famine and confusion. If all the people in the world were to live in their material civilization and living in the forests, the forest would then have to be transformed in to cities, else the inhabitants would die because lack of sanitation. On the other hand, material civilization is full of imperfections and misery.

Lord Siva (8th or 9th century) declares that God is the only reality and that creation is essentially an illusion. As man is, only the creature capable of conceiving of God, man himself must be divine, and his duty therefore is to realize his true nature.

Hinduism expressed the firm belief in natural environment in which man considered as manifestation of divine nature itself. Space (Akasa) considered first creation of Brahma. Akasa created air (Maruti or Vayu) and Vayu in the form of Tej or energy. The other element water and earth are further creations. It is the firm Hindu's belief that God resides in these various forms of Akasa, Vayu, Tej, water and earth created further entities. The Supreme is imminent every one of these components of environment.

The relationship between human beings and the earth is increasingly complicated and urgent. Air pollution, global warming and extinction of animal species that existing today. Religion is responding with views on the environment.

Human beings are the most intelligent life form on earth and are responsible for the damage that caused to the planet.

Hinduism is very concerned with the relationship between humanity and the environment. Karma teaches that resources in the world become scarce because people use them for their own ends. People should use the world unselfishly which results in natural imbalance and to repay God for the gifts he has given:

For, so sustained by sacrifice, the God will give you the food of your desire. Whose enjoys their gift, yet gives nothing, is a thief, no more nor less.

Bhagavad-Gita 3:12

Trees are treated with great respect, because it is the most important type of plant life and like all living things, has an atman (soul). If there is but one tree of flowers and fruit within a village, that place is worthy of your respect.

Fig.19: Banyan tree (Home for different creatures)

Mahabharata

The **God Krishna** compares the whole world with the **banyan tree** because it is so large and provides a home for many different creatures. The concept of ahimsa (non-violence and respect for life) prevents a Hindu from causing harm to any creature, and therefore, many Hindus are vegetarian.

In India, Hindus take an active part in checking government schemes which might damage the environment, such as the building of large-scale dams which could cause the rivers to flood, destroying precious land and animals.

The universe is the divine creation, and must be honored in all its parts. Animals and plants, mountains and rivers, all form part of the earth, and many are worshipped for the noble qualities they possess. Cows, for example are so highly revered that killing of them is banned and those that no longer produce milk are retired, not slaughtered and special sanctuaries called Goshallas have been created for them.

Ether, air, fire, water, earth, planets, all creatures, directions, trees and plants, rivers and seas--they all are organs of God's body. Remembering this, a devotee respects all species.

Srimad Bhagavata Mahapurana (2.2.41)

Karma:

An understanding of karma ties together these three grand concepts, informing us that our current condition is the combined product of our past actions (in this life and previous incarnations) and actions that we take today. In this way, we are constantly creating our future, in the months, years, decades and even lifetimes to come. Clearly, our actions also influence our family and community, today and into the future.

Consider climate change, one of the most pressing environmental issues of our time, as a lesson in karma. How did we cause greenhouse gas concentrations to rise so high that they are forcing myriad climatic changes? Through well over a century of burning fossil fuels, through cutting down forests and through increased rising of animals for meat. Many of our parents, grandparents and great-grandparents (to a lesser degree) all did this without thought of the future consequences. Indeed, it was not until the last decades of the 20th century that we began to recognize that there might be a long-term problem with this behavior. It is clear as day: we, the human race, created the threatening circumstances future generations and we now face. Our environmental karma is of our own creation.

4.2 HINDUISM: THE ORIGIN OF THE UNIVERSE:

Many of the world's religions have ideas and beliefs about the origin of the universe, including people and animals. Usually these take the form of creation accounts in the sacred books of the religions concerned.

The sacred sound **Aum** is believed to be the first sound at the start of creation. Hindus believe that Brahman (the one ultimate reality) has three functions, and these are shown by the three gods, Shiva, Brahma and Vishnu. These three are sometimes shown as three heads merging into one and are known as the **"Trimurti".**

- **Brahma** is the **Creator** and **source** of all creation.
- **Vishnu** is the Preserver and responsible for keeping all good things on earth.
- **Shiva** is the **Destroyer** and is needed because some things are **harmful** and because **change is necessary** for the creation of new things.

In the **Chandogya Upanishad** (A Hindu sacred text.) creation is described as the **breaking of an egg.**

In the Vedas (knowledge) one of the accounts says that the creator **built the universe with timber**, as a carpenter builds a house.

In the Rig Veda (the first scripture of Hinduism, containing spiritual and scientific knowledge) it says that the universe was created out of the parts of the body of a single cosmic man Purusha when his body was sacrificed.

There the four classes (varnas) of Indian society come from his body: the **priest** (Brahmin) from his mouth, the **warrior** (Kshatritya) from his arms, the **peasant** (Vaishya) from his thighs, and the **servant** (Shudra) from his legs.

The **Hymn of Creation**: Another attempt at explaining the creation of the universe is found in the Hymn of Creation in the Rig Veda:

Then was neither non-existence nor existence: there was no realm of air, no sky beyond it .Death was not then, nor was there anything immortal: no sign was there, the Day's and Night's divider.

Darkness there was: at first concealed in darkness this All was indiscriminate chaos. All that existed then was void and formless: by the great power of Warmth was born that One.

4.3 ORIGIN OF ENVIRONMENTAL SCIENCE FROM VEDAS:

The Vedas are the first texts in the library of humankind. They are universally acknowledged to be the most precious Indian Heritage. The Vedas deal with knowledge, the knowledge of all sorts.

They cover knowledge both physical and spiritual. They are source of all knowledge according to Manusmriti. The Vedic views revolve around the concept of nature and life. The visions of the beauty of life and nature in the Vedas are extremely rich in poetic value.

The most authoritative among the four Vedas is called the **Rig-Veda.** Each Vedic verse has one or more sages (Rishis) and deities (Devatas) associated with it. Generally, Rishis are supposed to be the recipient of knowledge revealed in the verses and Devatas are supposed to be the gods in whose praise verses are revealed.

In Vedic view, this world consists of Agni i.e., fire or heat and Soma i.e. water.

Sun (Surya) is the soul of all that is moving and of which is not moving.

Indra is most powerful God who kills Vritra, the symbol of cloud to free waters. Vritra meansone who covers and is derived from the root **vritra.** R.R.M. Roy opines that the main force of expansion in the Vedic cosmology is Indra, and his chief adversary, the main force of contraction, is Vritra.

Maruts are Indra's associates. Vedic seers pray boldly to these natural forces and aspects for bestowing plenty and prosperity on them.

The concept of the form of the **Earth** in the **Rig-Veda** is most fascinating.One of the mostbeautiful verse of the Rig-Veda says, 'Heaven is my father, brother atmosphere is my navel, and the great earth is my mother.' Earth is described as a goddess in **Rig-Veda**.

According to Rig-Veda, the water as a part of human environment occurs in **five** forms:

1. Rainwater (Divyah)
2. Natural spring (Sravanti)
3. Wells and canals (Khanitrimah)
4. Lakes (Svayamjah)
5. Rivers (Samudrarthah)

The significance of water for life was well known to Vedic seers. They mention–

- Waters are nectars.
- Waters are source of all plants and giver of good health.
- Waters destroy diseases of all sorts.
- Waters are for purification.

The **Padma Purana** condemns water pollution forcefully saying, 'the person who pollutes waters of ponds, wells or lakes goes to hell.' In Padma purana and karma purana, it is mentioned that the trees like, peepal, bel, ber, neem etc, are the abode of god and they are not to cut. This is nothing but a way of conserving the vegetation. Planting of trees and plants like **tulsi** in every house are considered religious acts. The puranas also recalls the virtues of plants and trees and stressed on the need to tree plantations. "The inhabitants of a house which has sacred basil (Ocimum sanctum) are fortunate" (Padam Puran 59.7). In Padma Puran (56.40-41) the cutting of a green tree is an offence punishable in hell.

The **Varah Purans** (172.39) says that "One who plants a peepal (Ficus religiosa), one neem (Azadirachta indica), one Banyan (Ficus benghalensis), two pomegranates (Punica granatum), two orange (Citrus reticulate), five mango trees (Mangifera indica) and ten flowering plants or creepers shall never go the hell".

Yajurveda says,' Vayu has penetrating brightness.' Apparent meaning of Vayu is air. The Yajurveda mentions about plants and animals, the ill effects of cutting of trees; and the poisoning of the atmosphere; but it also discusses about energy relations of the global ecosystem. "No persons should kill animals helpful to all" (Y.V. 13.37). "O King you should never kill animals like bullocks useful in agriculture or like cows which gives us milk and all other helpful animals and must punish those who kill or do harm to such animals" (Y.V. 13.49). The oceans are treasure of wealth protect them" (Y.V. 38.22); "Do not poison (pollute) water and do not harm or cut the trees (Y.V. 6.33); "Do not disturb the sky and do not poison the atmosphere" (Y.V. 5.43).

About the flow of energy in the global ecosystem, the Yajur Veda says "the whole universe is full of energy in which the sun is at the centre and the ultimate source of energy for all living organisms on earth. The net energy flows from the point of production to the point of consumption through the plants, animals, human beings, the air, water, land, and is completely under the control of Almighty. While energy flow and balance are maintained in the universe yet some imbalance this causes several natural disturbances like untimely rain, heavy rain, drought and flood, warm winter and cool summer.

Rig-Veda mentions 'O Air! You are our father, the protector'. Air has medicinal values.**'Let wind blow in the form of medicine and brings welfare and happiness.'**

Medicated air is the international physician that annihilates pollution and imparts health and hilarity, life and liveliness to people of the world. Hilly areas are full of medicated air consisted of herbal elements. The air is the soul of all deities. It exists in all as life-breath. It can move everywhere. We cannot see it. Only one can hear its sound.

Ancient Indians, therefore, emphasized that the unpolluted, pure air is source of good health, happiness, and long life. Pray Vayu (God) is to blow with its medicinal qualities. Sun shines in Divya- loka and we get light from sky. The sunrays strengthen our inner power and are essential for our Vedic verses.

The **Atharva Veda** mentions certain names of Oshadhis with their values. Later this information became important source for the **Ayurveda.** The **Rig-Veda** instructs that forests should not be destroyed.

The **Atharva Veda** talks about the relation of plants with earth. 'The earth is keeper of creation,container of forests, trees and herbs.' The Athrava Veda also mentions about the importance of air, water and green plants essential for human existence. Although there was as such no concept of the word "Pollution" those days, but it was referred in terms of "poisoning" of environment.

In accordance with Vedic approach to environment,It is clear that the Vedic vision to live in harmony with environment was not merely physical but was far wider and much comprehensive. The Vedic people desired to live a life of hundred years and this wish can be fulfilled only when environment will be unpolluted, clean and peaceful.

Essence of the environmental studies in the Vedas can be put here by quoting a partial Mantra of the **Ishavasyopanishad** 'One should enjoy with renouncing or giving up others part'.

Vedic message is clear that environment belongs to all living beings, so it needs protection by all, for the welfare of all.

Taittariya Upanishad (5.101) certain norms were prescribed for human beings to keep the environment clean. "One should not cause urine and stool in water, should not spit in water; and should not take bath without clothes". The **Iso-Upanishad** has revealed the secrets of existence of life on earth and the importance of every organism for mutual survival. "The universe along with its creatures belongs to the Lord. No creation is superior to any other.

All four major Vedas 'the Rig, Sama, Yajur and Atharva Vedas' recognize the importance of maintenance of the seasons' cycles that are likely to get altered due to the climate change owing to inappropriate human actions. It is remarkable that the people in Vedic times regarded Nature and the environment in a holistic manner and revered each of its constituents and entities by carefully preserving them. "Do not harm the environment; do not harm the water and the flora; earth is my mother, I am her son; may the waters remain fresh, do not harm the waters... Tranquility be to the atmosphere, to the earth, to the waters, to the crops and vegetation." This Vedic prayer invokes divine intervention to bless and protect the environment.

4.4 THE TEACHINGS OF ATHARVA VEDA:

"Let there be peace in the heavens, the Earth, the atmosphere, the water, the herbs, the vegetation, among the divine beings and in Brahman, the absolute reality. Let everything be at peace and in peace. Only then will we find peace."-Atharva Veda.

Atharva Veda is Indian scripture wherein the concept of respect for earth has pronounced. Further, Rig-Veda regarded plants as have dative power. Many verses in these Vedas have devoted in the praise of Lord Surya Devata, Vayu Devata, Agni Devata, Varun Devata, Mother Earth, Vana Devi, etc. Accordingly, felling of trees, polluting air, water, and desert land regarded as sin as these were respected and regarded as God and Goddess. Maintaining these pure was the duty of everyone.

Our ancestors considered it as their pious duty to save trees and every tree have religious sanctity.

The sages of the Atharva Veda chanted:

"What of thee I dig out,
Let that quickly grow over,
Let me not hit thy vital, or
Thy heart"(Ramjilal,56).

This means that one can take from the earth and atmosphere only so much as one put back to them. In the present days, this considered one of the most important principles of sustainable development. The purity and quality of water has been highlighted in the Atharva Veda. It is mentioned that pure water cures many ailments, and it acts as preventer of the diseases, which are not yet contracted. Atharva Veda speaks about the protection of wildlife and domestic cattle. The cattle were meant to adorn the ceremony but not for sacrifice.

Trees and plants had regarded as indispensable in the life of human being and considered as the abode of various Gods and Goddesses, cited here under.

Hindu declarations on Climate Change:

[Presented for Consideration to the Convocation of Hindu Spiritual Leaders Parliament of the World's Religions, Melbourne, Australia, December 8, 2009]

Earth, in which the seas, the rivers and many waters lie, from which arise foods and fields of grain, abode to all that breathes and moves, may she confer on us Her finest yield. ---Bhumi Suktam, Atharva Veda xii.1.3.

The Hindu tradition understands that man is not separate from nature, that spiritual, psychological and physical bonds with the elements around us link us. Knowing that the Divine is present everywhere and in all things, Hindus strive to do no harm. We hold a deep reverence for life and an awareness that the great forces of nature—the earth, the water, the fire, the air and space—as well as all the various orders of life, including plants and trees, forests and animals, are bound to each other within life's cosmic web.

Our beloved Earth, so touchingly looked upon as the Universal Mother, has nurtured mankind through millions of years of growth and evolution. Now centuries of rapacious exploitation of the planet have caught up with us, and a radical change in our relationship with nature is no longer an option. It is a matter of survival. We cannot continue to destroy nature without also destroying ourselves. The dire problems besetting our world—war, disease, poverty and hunger—will all be magnified many fold by the predicted impacts of climate change.

The nations of the world have yet to agree upon a plan to ameliorate man's contribution to this complex change. This is largely due to powerful forces in some nations which oppose any such attempt, challenging the very concept that unnatural climate change is occurring. Hindus everywhere should work toward an international consensus. Humanity's very survival depends upon our capacity to make a major transition of consciousness, equal in significance to earlier transitions from nomadic to agricultural, agricultural to industrial and industrial to technological. We must transit to complementarily in place of competition, convergence in place of conflict, holism in place of hedonism, optimization in place of maximization. We must, in short, move rapidly toward a global consciousness that replaces the present fractured and fragmented consciousness of humans.

Mahatma Gandhi urged, "You must be the change you wish to see in the world." If alive today, he would call upon Hindus to set the example, to change our lifestyle, to simplify our needs and restrain our desires.

Diversity in nature complements itself, i.e., every component complements another. In the words of Mahatma Gandhi, "There is enough for every man's need, but not every man's greed." Nature has created enough to meet the requirements of every living creature, but there is an essential element of give-and-take that we cannot forget. We must remember that, sacrifice and enjoyment are two sides of the same coin. Today, however, we have erroneously set our sights on enjoyment alone, and avoid any form of giving-back. Our enjoying benefits without contributing back to the environment are tantamount to theft.

This spirit of give-and-take is also underscored in a verse from the **Ishavasyopanishad** that mandates that only after contributing productively should one seek gratification. This is the most fundamental tenet of environmental conservation.

As one sixth of the human family, Hindus can have a tremendous impact. We can and should take the lead in Earth-friendly living, personal frugality, lower power consumption, alternative energy, sustainable food production and vegetarianism, as well as in evolving technologies that positively address our shared plight.

Hindus recognize that it may be too late to avert drastic climate change. Thus, in the spirit of vasudhaiva kutumbakam, "the whole world is one family," Hindus encourage the world to be prepared to respond with compassion to such calamitous challenges as population displacement, food and water shortage, catastrophic weather, and rampant disease.

Sanatana Dharma envisions the vastness of God's manifestation and the immense cycles of time in which it is perfectly created, preserved, and destroyed, again and again, every dissolution being the preamble to the next creative impulse. Notwithstanding this spiritual reassurance, Hindus still know we must do all that is humanly possible to protect the Earth and her resources for the present as well as future generations.

4.5 TREES ASSOCIATED WITH THE GODS & GODDESSES:

Sr.No.	Name of Tree/Plant	Name of the God / Goddess
1	Asvatha	Vishnu, Laxmi
2	Vata	Brahma, Vishnu, Kuber
3	Tulsi	Vishnu, Laxmi, Purvaja
4	Soma	Chandra (Moon)
5	Bel	Lord Shiva
6	Ashoka	Buddha, Indra
7	Amlaki	Laxmi, Karthik, Urvarak, Dharmik, Upashna
8	Tal	Buddha Ataman, Mrit Ataman (Bhoot)
9	Amra	Laxmi, Govardhan, Urvarak, Oharmik, Upashna
10	Kadamb	Krishna, Urvarak, Dharmik, Upashna Vidhi
11	Neem	Shitla, Manas, Chudail
12	Palash	Brahma, Gandharva
13	Pipal	Vishnu, Krishna, Purvaja
14	Mahnu	Urvarak, Dharmik, Upashna Vidhi
15	Semal	Urvarak, Dharmik, Upashna Vidhi
16	Aakh	Urvarak, Dharmik, Upashna Vidhi
17	Narikel (coconut)	Urvarak, Dharmik, Upashna Vidhi
18	Phig	Vishnu, Rudra

19	Karpur	Chandra
20	Shiora	Vana Durga, Laxmi
21	Sij	Shitla
22	Tamal	Krishna

Among Hindus, trees worshipped as Vana Devata (tree deity) with prayers offering of water, flower, and sweets and encircled by sacred threads. Planting of trees treated as sacred religious duty and work of great virtue and regarded one tree to equal ten sons.

Varaha Purana says: One who plants one pipal, one neem, one ber, ten flowering plant creepers, two pomegranates, two oranges and five mango trees; they will not go to hell.

4.6 CHARAKA SAMHITA:

Charka Samhita has considered that the destruction of forests as the most dangerous act for humanity and its welfare. The destruction of forests is most dangerous for the nation and for human beings. Vanaspati (vegetation) has direct relationship with the well-being of the society.

Due to the pollution of natural environment and the destruction of Vanaspati, many diseases crop up to ruin the nation.

The Charaka Samhita (III.6.23) discusses in detail disease-causing effects of polluted and disturbed air, water, land, and seasons as a cause of destruction of entire countries. Twenty-eight factors of damage to air, water and land are listed, of which we can find all occurring in the world today. Besides harmful factors to the outer world, they include perverse and selfish behavior on the part of human beings, their fall from ethical behavior and disregard for spiritual practices, particularly unrighteous conduct by the rulers of a country and above allviolence and war.

Charaka Samhitha states that when natural time cycles, as if the seasons become disrupted, the situation becomes most dangerous. Also states that such collective problems and diseases can be avoided and countered by health practices like pancha karma, by a sattvic life and the practices of yoga and meditation. Clearly our disruption of the environment has consequences both material and spiritual nature, though these may take some more decades to fully manifest, as nature works on a slower time cycle than human beings. One must reconnect ourselves with universal peace and once more come to honor the Earth and nature in order to solve this dire situation.

4.7 MANU (MANUSMRITI):

Manusmriti composed originally before 3000 B.C. by Manu, a mythical sage and the first

King of divine origin in India. Among the Dharmasastras (law books) in ancient India, the text known as Manusmriti occupies a very important place because of its wide coverage and detailed guidelines for various aspects of human living.

Manusmriti is otherwise known as Manav Dharma Sastra (compendium of human principles)with a basic theme that Dharma (Principle) is not religion (the so called belief or cult followed by a specific group, may be based on a specific personality or dogma) and it has created a vista for the human society, may not be specifically alone for the Aryans of the ancient India.

Maharshi Manu (Manu Vaivasswata) a renowned yogi: a man of wisdom and great elite of Vedas:

the saver and conservator of biodiversity during dissolution. Manusmruti from ethnobiological point of view since1995 (Dash, 1998; Padhy, 2000) and also exposing (Padhy et al., 1996, 1999, 2001) have provided enough scope to realize that the ancient Indian environmental and ethical education deserves a rediscovery and needs an ecological implementation in the new millennium at par.

Human environment is divided into six categories as follows:

a) Socio-ecological niche
b) Academic environment
c) Family Atmosphere
d) Social Interaction
e) Salubrity: An environmental necessity.
f) Ethical protection for biota

The ecological principles of Manusmriti based on the basic ideal of the Upanishads, "Vasudhaiva -kutumbakam", i.e., all the beings of the entire universe belong to the same family. By means of defining cosmology, Manu here endeavors to spell out the basic sources of Interrelationship among all beings in this universe. Manu describes how all the material (and perishable) things (living beings as well as lifeless matters) of the world have originated from the same five elements or Pancha-bhutas [Khiti (Earth), Ap (Water), Teza (Fire), Marut(Air) and Byom (Sky)]. Manu provides guidelines for harmonious living with the orderly universe. In this regard, Manu prescribes various rites to get rid of the sin committed to nature and its universal ecology. Here looks upon all these matters from moral and religious standards. Manu describes the religious consequences of killing, destroying or injuring various types of living-beings. This was intended to preserve bio-diversity.

In this way, Manu's approach towards preservation of environment and ecology was a holistic one, where he treated this as a part of the cosmic harmony.

The Code of Manu (Manusmriti) which had held uninterrupted sway over the Hindu way of life all through the post Vedic period lays down in the minutes detail the duties performed by the different functional groups in their day to day conduct in order to maintain a happy state of material welfare, peace and harmony. Similarly, Yajnyavalka Smriti spells out man's obligation towards the protection of the plants and animal kingdom for his own survival and prosperity. However, the idea of material progress in India centered on the felling of mangala. It encompasses of feeling of general welfare, well being and prosperity put together. The Vedic seers who had the realization of the Supreme reality have found the presence of that reality in all entities. The surroundings in which the very compassionate Lord places man are divine in nature and are the very manifestations of that supreme principle. The earth, the sky, the air, the ire, the winds, the mountains, the rivers, the night, the dawn, the birds, the trees and the plants, the forests have all been defined. Man's well being depends on all these divinities directly and it considered his duty to respect and revere these in all sincerity and to refrain from any injury of insult to these.

In the Manusmriti it is stated that the yajna or sacrificial fire is the cause of biological evolution. In Manusmriti the cruelty towards animals has been condemned. It is stated that the killer of the cattle is doomed to die as many times as there are hair on the skin of the cattle. It is further stated that even after death, he shall have no peace. Manusmriti also mentions about the optimum use of the resources of the nature. This is yet another way to maintain the ecosystem. Certain trees are considered to be scared and they are worshiped. They are not to be cut.

The Hindu way of life and respect and consideration for natural world including for animals and birds the most important aspect of the Hindu mythology was the association accorded to different species with reincarnation and duties. It was believed that Supreme Being has actually gets himself incarnated in the form of various species. Further Hindu philosophy was to treat all other species just their children. One should look upon deer, camels, monkeys, rats, reptiles, birds, and flies as though they were their own children, what is that distinguished these from those (children).

4.8 ANIMALS ASSOCIATED WITH GOD/ GODDESS:

Several Hindu Gods and Goddesses have animals and birds as their associates. The selective examples are as follows:

Name of God/Goddess	Associated Animals/birds
Durga	Lion
Brahma	Wild goose
Indra	Elephant
Ganesh	Rat
Shiva	Bull, Serpent, Snake
Saraswati	Swan, Peacock
Vishnu	Eagle
Kama	Fish
Rama Hanuman	Monkey
Kartikeya	Peacock
Laxmi	Owl
Ganga	Crocodile
Sitla	Ass

Bhairava	Dog
Vayu	Deer

4.9 TEACHINGS OF YAJURVED:

In the "Yajurveda" killing of animals prohibited and observed that no person should kill animals. One should be helpful to all animals and by serving these one would obtain heaven. In the Code of Manu i.e., Manusmriti, it has observed that he who injures innocuous being with a desire to give him pleasure, never finds happiness, neither living nor dead.

Killing of animals is against basic tenet of Hindu way of life that has deep faith in the doctrine of Ahimsa (non-violence) Therefore, one should not kill Gods creatures but should protect these and Killing of mute animals and birds still considered a sin.

Yajurveda dealt with many human rights factors. Right to truth was a component to humanity. Even, the Yajurveda dreamed Amaratva, the survival forever. The Environment is called as Devayajaní in Yajurveda. Here, the natural phenomenon like earth, Varuṇa, vāyu etc. are the upholders of moral order. Man has given the competence and right for its conservation and growth, which would promote his own survival.

Right and duty are like the two sides of a same coin. Hence, Veda sponsored the right to the people, subject to condition with their reciprocal duties and conducts towards the society. No rights could be claimed without the proper duties.

4.10 BISHOIN'S FAITH AND ENVIRONMENT PROTECTION:

Bishnoie is a distinct sect of Hindus who treated environment protection as a part of their religious duty. Guru Jambheshwar have new message of love and peace adding fresh dimension human consciousness, enlarging man's vision of the Universe and Cosmic life. He propounded 29 principles, which deal with specific aspects of life. In the deserts Rajasthan, there has always been a feeling of oneness between nature and Bislmois. Bishnoi's history tells us that in the year of 1730, near Jodhpur in Rajasthan in Khejris village 365 Bhishnoi's gave up their lives to safeguard the Khejri trees and led by a woman Mrs. Amerita Bai. They guarded trees. The men of the king kept felling the trees and side by side, they too axed.

Sunder lal Bahuguna has become an internationally well-known example of a highly successful conservation action program through the efforts of local people for guarding their forest resources in India known to be 'chipko-movement'. Bishnoi's faith preaches that trees are brothers and sisters. Before going to daily business, they would salute the trees. Children are educated not to harm the trees.

Thus, according to Bishnoi's faith we have a culture that trees regarded as more precious and revered as lives. Recently, the film stars from Bollywood handed over to the police by Bishnoi's of Rajasthan while hunting the animals is a fine example of protecting the wildlife by a religious group.

In India, environmental protection not only merely confined to religious preaching but also finds place in the ancient literature. Kalidas, the greatest of the Indian poets, sang in the praises of Himalayas in 'Meghdoot' by describing it as the loftiest mountain on the earth surface located on the north of the country. The Himalayan ranges have influenced the climate, culture, ecology and environment of subcontinent. These are the ranges, where originate several perennial rivers like, the Ganga and the Yamuna, has become a fertile part of India. The legendary tradition of our culture is deeply associated with these two rivers as rightly observed by the Apex Court of India.

4.11 HINDUISM AND ECOLOGY:

Hinduism has long revered the tree. Early seals from the Indus Valley cities (ca. 3000 BCE) depict the tree as a powerful symbol of abundance. References to India's trees can be found in a wide range of literature, particularly in epic and poetic texts.

India has a long history of forest protection, from the edicts of Asoka to the individual work of various Rajas, to the modern Chipko movement, wherein women have staved off forest destruction by surrounding trees with their own bodies.

Rivers have been and continue to be an integral part of Hindu religious practice. More than fifty Vedic hymns praise the Sarasvati, a river (now dry) associated with the goddess of learning and culture. The Ganges River, which flows through northern India, likewise is referred to as a goddess originating from the top of Siva's head in the Himalaya Mountains, giving sustenance to hundreds of millions of modern Indians. Traditionally, the rivers of India have always considered pure. Modern industrial contaminants and human wastes have fouled the rivers, though Ganges water still plays an important role in India's ritual life.

Hinduism offers a variety of cosmological views that may or may not situate the human in the natural world in an ecologically friendly manner. On the one hand, the agrarian and often near-wilderness images of India found in the Vedas, Upanishads, and epic texts present a style of life seemingly in tune with the elements. The Samkhya and Tantra traditions affirm the reality and efficacy of the physical world. On the other hand, the *Advaita Vedanta* tradition, while adopting the basic principles of Samkhya cosmology, asserts that the highest truth involves a vision of oneness that transcends nature and, in a sense, dismisses the significance of the material world by referring to it as illusion or Maya.

One model of Hindu spirituality encourages physicality through yoga practices that enhance the health of the body and the vitality of the senses. Other spiritual paths advocate renunciation of all sensual attachments to the world. However, even within the paths that relegate worldly concerns to a status of secondary importance, the doctrine of *Dharma* emphasizes a need to act "for the sake of the good of the world." Particularly concerning such issues as the building of dams in the Narmada River Valley, this requires considering social ecology or the need to integrate environmental policy with the daily needs of tribal and other marginalized peoples.

The current worldwide ecological crisis has only emerged during the past four decades and its effects have felt within South Asia more recently. As the region copes with decreasing air quality in its cities and degraded water in various regions, religious thinkers and activists have begun to reflect on how the broader values of Hindu tradition might contribute to fostering greater care for the earth. Gandhi's advocacy of simple living through the principles of nonviolence (*ahimsa*) and holding to truthfulness (*Satyagraha*) could give some Hindus pause as they consider the lifestyle changes engendered by contemporary consumerism. Most of the Hindu population lives within villages that, barring natural disasters such as flood or drought, are self-sustaining and use resources sparingly. However, as the population of South Asia increases, and as the modern lifestyle continues to demand consumer goods, the balance of sustainability can shatter. With appreciation and acknowledgment of the five great elements, with a new interpretation of social duty (*dharma*) expanded to include the ecological community, and with remembrance of its ethic of abstemiousness, the Hindu tradition can develop new modalities for caring for the earth.

****

Chapter-5

BUDDHISM

5.1. Buddhism and environmental Protection, 5.2 The Teachings of Buddha, 5.3 Environmental Buddhism in Practice, 5.4 Environmental Monks, 5.5 Phra Prajak (Environmental Monks), 5.6 Great Emperor Ashoka

5.1 BUDDHISM AND ENVIRONMENTAL PROTECTION:

Buddhism is a religion that places great emphasis on environmental protection. Sakyamuni Buddha was born at Lumbini Garden. Mahamaya Devi gave birth to Siddhartha only after holding a branch of tree. Siddhartha at 35 year's old attained enlightenment under a tree, which became popular in the name of Bodhi tree (tree of enlightenment). After getting enlightenment, he became so grateful to the Boddhi tree that he with profound gratitude gazed Bodhi tree with motion less eyes for one whole week.

He engaged in spiritual practice in the forest, attained Buddha hood under a tree, and first began preaching at Deer Park.

Buddhism came into existence as religion by the end of Vedic period. Buddhism is the pinnacle of the world's philosophy and that it provides the greatest enjoyment for humankind. The fundamental tenets of the Buddhism are truth, non-violence, **respect and love for living organism including trees and plants. Buddhism also emphasized very much over the rational use of natural resources by the man.**

Simplicity and non-violence are the two cardinal principles of Buddhism. These are closely inter-related. The optimal pattern of consumption, producing a high degree of human satisfaction by means of a relatively low rate of consumption allows people to live without pressure and strain and to fulfill the primary injunction of Buddhist teaching cease to do evil, try to do well.

Buddha a great teacher, said as the pioneer in protection of the physical as well as mental environment. According to Buddha, actual up grading the life of people is possible only by protecting physical and mental environment of the people.

Buddha has given importance of proper environment to get success in physical as well as spiritual development. According to him the overall development of a people start from the environment, he is living in. In Mangala (Auspice) sutra, Buddha had said that "**Patirupa desh vaso caetam mangala mutttamam**". The meaning is "It is auspice to live at the proper place". Proper place here means the place with good environment. Good environment include less polluted place, with protection of nature, having necessary opportunity of good education, medical cure, employment facilities and opportunity of spiritual practice. It is obvious that one can live and get success easily physically as well as spiritually, if he is inhabitants of good environment.

Buddha not only inspired people to preserve environment, but he also himself had shown the activities for preserving it. Buddha emphasized not only to abate physical pollution which is cause due to destruction of physical environment, he emphasized also to protect social psychological and moral environment.

5.2 THE TEACHINGS OF BUDDHA

Ancient Buddhist teachings says that the earth is a great-enlightened being, a great "**Bodhisattva**" gives us a place to live on her body to grow and to walk the path to enlightenment. The earth is the mother of all beings that live upon her. "**Since all of those beings have the same mother as we do, they are all our own brothers and sisters".**

"Heaven is father and earth is mother". The ultimate way to rescue the environment is to return to a state of innocence and truth, and not to engage in fighting, selfishness, avarice, and deceit.

The Teaching of Buddha enjoys in a reverent and non-violent attitude not only to all sentient beings but has also emphasized on trees. Every follower of Buddha ought to plant a tree every few years and look after it until it is safely established.

The Buddha told in the sutras and precepts that one should take loving care of animals, and should not harm the grass and trees, but regard them as the home where sentient beings lead their lives. In the stories of the Buddha's past lives, when he was following the Bodhisattva path, he was once reborn as a bird. During a forest fire, he tried fearlessly to put out the fire, disregarding his own safety by bringing water with his feathers.

In the Avatamsaka Sutra, it is said that mountains, waters, grass, and trees are all the manifestation of the great bodhisattvas. Therefore, Buddhists believe that both sentient beings and non-sentient things are all the Dharma-body of the Buddha's. Therefore, Buddhists regard our living environment as their own bodies.

Buddhists believe in the principle of Karma that states, "Every cause has an effect." With this view of the world one is prompted to care about the impacts of one's actions on all that surrounds them, including the environment. Five Precepts guide the Buddhist along the path of enlightenment. Three of these can apply directly to conservation: Do not harm any living creature; Do not take more than you need; and Do not act thoughtlessly.

"The entire cosmos is a cooperative. The sun, the moon, and the stars live together as a cooperative. The same is true for humans and animals, trees, and the earth. When we realize that the world is a mutual, interdependent, cooperative enterprise then we can build a noble environment. If our lives are not based on this truth, then we shall perish." - **Buddhadasa Bhikkhu.**

The immoderate development and the excessive use of chemicals in the world have led to the rapid consumption of natural resources, the speedy deterioration of the natural environment, and the extinction of a variety of species. The collective result speeds the earth towards doomsday. Although no human being hopes for the early arrival of doomsday, few are willing to strive together to take action to salvage the destiny of the earth, despite the fact that most are conscious of the crisis. Day in and day out everyone still consumes even larger amounts of natural resources, produces more refuse to pollute the earth, the air, and rivers and oceans. The remaining tracts of tropical rain forest become smaller and smaller; the number of species likewise decreases, and desertification of the land expands at a faster rate. If this situation is not placed in check and reversed, then humankind will have become extinct even before the earth is destroyed.

Buddha's teaching of "leading a contented life with few desires" and "being satisfied and therefore always happy", and if we are willing to use our intelligence to deal with problems and engage diligently in productive work, then, without having to contend with one another or fight with nature, we can lead very happy lives.

Therefore, the members of our organization use the following four sentences to encourage one another:Our needs are little; Our wants are great. Pursue only what we really need; What we want is unimportant.

Dharma Drum Mountain, small Buddhist community of only about one million members, has in the last ten years promoted four major principles of environmental protection:

1. The cherishing of natural resources and the protection of the ecological environment.
2. Maintaining cleanliness in family life and using daily necessities simply and frugally.
3. Improving interpersonal politeness and social etiquette and,
4. Instead of considering everything from the standpoint of one person, one race, one time-period, and one place, we should consider it from the standpoint that all humankind of all time and space should be protected in their existence, possess the right to live, and feel the dignity of life.

In brief, the above-mentioned four kinds of environmentalism can be re- stated as natural environmentalism, lifestyle environmentalism, social etiquette environmentalism, and spiritual environmentalism.

Environmental protection must be combined with our respective religious beliefs and philosophical thinking into an earnest mission, so that environmentalism will not become mere slogans. Therefore, strictly speaking, the purification of humankind's mind and heart is more important than the purification of the environment. If our mind is free from evil intentions and cannot be polluted by the surroundings, our living environment will also not be spoiling and polluted by us. However, for ordinary people, it is advisable to set out by cultivating the habit of protecting the material environment and go deeper gradually until at last they can cultivate environmentalism on the spiritual level.

There are several teachings of the protection of trees in the Buddhist literature as in Vinaya pitaka, Jataka, Dharma pada, petavatthu etc. There are several rules in Vinaya pitaka which prohibit monks to make pollutions.

Buddha's teachings emphasize to make good mentality in order to get peace of mind. The first verse of Dharma pada states mind as the forerunner of states. Mind is chief; mind -made are they. All the activities are based on the mind so if mind is polluted several problems would arise and if mind is free from pollution environment becomes so pure that everyone will be able to enjoy calm and peace.

Buddha had said that good or bad environment is also the product of the vibration produced by people living at the place. The people who are free from defilements produce good vibration; the place would be cheerful and peaceful where the saintly person without defilement lives. It is because every person produces mental vibration in the atmosphere creating good or bad environment. Therefore, the place would be delightful if there are people living with good vibration and vice versa.

According to Buddha, mental vibration has powerful effect in making the environment delightful. Only making good environment physically is not sufficient, people inhabitants should also possess good mentality in order to make the place delightful. One cannot live happily and peacefully at that place if the majority of people there are full of anger, hatred and illusions. However, people even with full of tension can feel happy and peace if the place is full with loving kindness, compassion, sympathetic joy and equanimity. In this way, a person with good mentality can contribute for the good environment in the society.

Buddha had inspired to make good environment because it helps to get success in social life, economic life and spiritual life. If the teachings of Buddha are propagated properly, the problem of environmental destruction can be minimized significantly.

Animals and Birds are given equal important in the Buddhist literature. Buddha had taken several births as animals and birds and had performed several welfare activities for their community. Five precepts which are basic teachings of Buddha prohibit killing and slaughtering the animals.

In accordance with the spirit of the Buddhist percepts, all over the world, one should abstain from killing animal either for pastime or for sacrifice. In the ancient India before the birth of Buddhism, the slaughtering of animals for sacrifices was common. Buddhism is not only abhorring the vein destruction of animal life, but also regarded it as his duty to care for the well-being of all animals.

5.3 ENVIRONMENTAL BUDDHISM IN PRACTICE:

A handful of Thai monks consider themselves as "**environmental monks**" (*Pharanak anuraksa thammachat in Thai*). They work to protect the natural environment, setting up wildlife refuges and community forests, and fighting deforestation and environmental degradation, all based on their interrelations of Buddhist teachings. Their work often brings them into conflict with businesspersons, entrepreneurs and government officials who aim to use land to improve the nation's economy through schemes such as commercial and hydroelectric dams to power the new developments.

Claiming a moral high ground because of their status as monks and their use of Buddhist principles, these monks must act in a mundane world in which they affect, and affected by, secular law and economic concerns. On one level, environmental monks must have a solid grounding in Buddhist philosophy that justifies their actions in terms of religious and ecclesiastical regulations.

In Dharmapada monks are instructed to live in the village without disturbing the people and without making pollution by giving an example of "Bee".

As a bee without harming the flower, its color or scent, flies away, collecting only the honey, even so should the sage wander in the village." The great concerned of Buddha in the protection of tree is also depicted in this verse of Dharmapada where Buddha had said: "Cut down the unnecessary brush (of the passion) but not a single tree. It has a great significant meaning in the sense that we should protect trees from unnecessary and unwanted bushes and grass, which may hamper actual growth of the trees. It also signifies that we should cleanse impurities of our mind to achieve purity.

5.4 ENVIRONMENTAL MONKS:

All members of the sangha uphold ecological principles to the extent of protecting the environment within their temples and following the vinaya rules. The term "**environmental monk**" however refers to the few monks who consciously use Buddhist principles to preserve the natural environment of the society in which they live. Their activities range from studying the scriptural roots of conservation and adapting traditional rituals in order to promote ecological awareness to leading protest against environmental destruction and forming environmentally conscious development organizations.

They sponsor activities to preserve the natural environment and help people whose livelihood based on exploitation of it to find alternative and sustainable means if surviving. They base their activities in interpretations of Buddhist principles that emphasize the inter-connectedness of all beings and the responsibilities of humans towards the larger environment.

Many of today's monks participate in these trends themselves. Men join the sangha for several reasons. Some genuinely called to religious practice. Others see the sangha as a means of social promotion, as they instantly gain high social status. Others view the monk hood as an easy livelihood, as the laity takes care of their material needs. Duncan Mc Cargo (2004) argues that the majority of Thai monks ordain for social material reasons, and that the sangha as a whole has degenerated. He points out that the main activities of contemporary monks involve fund raising and performing ceremonies.

In this context of raising farmer debt and an increasing number of monks is struggling to maintain the relevance of the religion in today's society, and to counter the negative effects of consumerism and materialism. Environmental monks optimize these efforts, and the risks they are willing to take on in the name of social justice.

5.5 PHRA PRAJAK (ENVIRONMENTAL MONKS):

Perhaps the best-known environmental monk during the early 1990s was Phra Prajak Kuttajitto. A forest monk living in the woods of Northeastern Thailand (Isan), Phra Prajak emerged onto the public stage in 1991 (Tailor 1993, 1996:39-46). Through his practice and life in the forests of Isan, Prajak became aware of negative social and environmental effects of Government and military sponsored development schemes. His controversial efforts to protect forest reserves and help villagers impacted by those schemes led to him twice arrested and imprisoned for allegedly violating state laws.

At the same time, Phra Prajak was fighting Government and involvement in the controversial and social effects, Ajahn Pongsak worked in Northern Thailand to help villagers reclaim degraded agricultural land and fought to protect watershed regions from mountain agriculture. He founded the Dhammanaat foundation for conservation and rural development in 1983, aimed at supporting forest conservation and development according to the principles of morality, and helping local people (read lowland Thais) to practice dharma and develops their communities in ways that do not harm the natural environment on which they depend.

5.6 GREAT EMPEROR ASHOKA:

Emperor Ashoka, who ruled over more than two thirds of the Indian subcontinent, suffered great remorse for the suffering that he had caused, banned the killing of animals and exhorted his subjects to lead kind and tolerant lives. He also promoted tolerance towards all religions, which he supported financially. The prevalent religions of that time were the sramanas or wandering ascetics, Brahmins, Ajivakas and Jains. He recommended that all religions desist from self-praise and condemnation of others. His pronouncements were written on rocks at the periphery of his kingdom and on pillars along the main roads and where pilgrims gathered. He also established many hospitals for both humans and animals. King Ashoka wanted the non-violence to be the cultural heritage of the people. Therefore, punishment was prescribed for killing animals.

Some of his important rock edicts stated:

1. Asoka ordered that banyan trees and mango groves be planted, rest houses built and wells dug every half mile along the main roads.
2. He ordered the end to killing of any animal for use in the royal kitchens.
3. He ordered the provision of medical facilities for humans and beasts.
4. He commanded obedience to parents, generosity to priests and ascetics and frugality in spending.
5. All officers must work for the welfare of the poor and the aged.
6. He recorded his intention to promote the welfare of all beings in order to repay his debt to all beings.
7. He honors men of all faiths.

Buddhists abstain from taking life, not because, as they believe in the transmigration of souls, but solely through compassion and oblige. Buddhism inculcates compassion for animal life. The Buddhist follower emperor Great Ashoka promoted the planting and preservation of flora and fauna. He prescribed various punishments for hunting the creatures, like, ants, squirrels, rats, birds and for cutting of trees. He established two kinds of hospitals, one for men and another for beasts.

****

Chapter - 6

JAINISM, SIKHISM, JUDAISM & JEWISH ENVIRONMENTAL PROTECTION

6.1 JAINISM AND ENVIRONMENTAL PROTECTION:

Jain religion maintaining harmony between men an nature, man and man but lays down even greater stress on minimum destruction of living and non-living resources for man's satisfaction of material needs. Ahimsa is the foundation of the Jain religion. Jainism prohibits the eating of any kinds of meat. In Jainism Ahimsa given the greatest importance and has been called the highest virtue (Paramodhemah).

For a Jainist the fifteen vows should be renounced, some vows are related to the environment protection. In Jainism vows known as Karmas, namely, Vankark, Sphotrk Karma, Nirlanchan Karma and Asatipashan Kann related to the environment.

Although the final goal of Jainism transcends earthly concerns, Jainism is, in essence, a religion of ecology, of a sustainable lifestyle, and of reverence for life. Their religion's entire emphasis is on life consonant with ecology. Jain people can use their experience of applying non-violent principles in meeting the present ecological needs. Their religion presents a worldview that stresses the interrelatedness of all forms of life (Jiva). Its attendant ethics, which based on obligations, might easily extended to embrace an earth ethics.

The Jeeva is respected. As a highly evolved form of life, human beings have great moral responsibility in their mutual dealings and relationships with the rest of the universe. This ethical responsibility made the Jain tradition a cradle for the creed of environmental protection and harmony. Jainism is a religion of compassion- it aims at the welfare of all living beings. An important principle of Jainism expressed in Sutrakarta-anga as follows: "**A man should wander about treating all creatures as he himself would be treated**." Inflicting an injury to other beings is inflicting injury to oneself.

Ahimsa is the concept of non-violence, the injunction of not harming living beings. It is one of the foremost doctrines of Jainism. It has emerged from the doctrine of the equality of all souls. It grew from the belief in reincarnation: a person might come back in the form of an animal or insect, no living creature ever harmed.

As in Buddhism, and Hinduism, Jain ethics assert that any violence has harmful effects on those who commit it, with consequent ill effects in terms of Karma.

"**Ahimsa-Paramo-Dharmah**," **non-injury to living beings,** is one of the basic virtues. To kill a living being is the greatest of sins. Flowing from the Jain principle of non-violence is the tenet of reverence for all life – not just human life but extending to animal life and, in theory, even to the vegetable kingdom. Jains' practice of non-violence fosters an attitude of respect for all life forms. All living beings regarded as equal. Jainism insists that there must be no destruction responsibly considered. There should be compassion of all beings at every step of daily life. For the Jains ahimsa has come to embody ones willingness to separate oneself not merely from acts of injury or killing, but also from the entire mechanism of aggression, possession, and consumption that is so common in the world. To prevent even accidental damage to creatures, Jains may wear nose masks to prevent inhalation of insects. They may sweep the ground clear ahead of them. Some do not wash for fear of killing body lice or other parasites. Although Jain laypeople might participate in tree planting projects, their nuns and monks likely would not. This is because of the harm that caused to the earth, earthworms, and other forms of life during the digging process.

Jain laypersons enjoined to engage in occupations that are not associated with violence and/or destruction of life and follow a vegetarian diet. Animal sacrifice forbidden: There is the story of **yashodara** who went to hell because of his innately violent disposition: he offered to a goddess a cockerel, and it did not count that the bird was merely made of dough. The doctrine of ahimsa gives Jainism (as well as Buddhism and Hinduism) a strong pacifist streak. Among other characteristics of the Jain tradition are conservation and particularly "**Anckantavada**" (non-one-sidedness): this philosophy states that no single perspective on any issue contains the whole truth. It emphasizes the concept of universal independence.

6.2 JAINISM&ECOLOGY:

The Jains tradition has existed in tandem with Hinduism in India since at least 800 BCE. Whereas the Hindu faith looks to the Vedas for texts and rituals and to the Brahman caste for religious leadership, the Jains developed their own sacred texts (including the Acaranga Sutra, ca. 300 BCE) and follow the authority of itinerant monks and nuns who wander throughout India preaching the essential principles and practices of the faith. As indicated above, Hinduism includes both monistic and dualistic theologies, with several variations of each. Jains ascribe to the belief in plural life forms populating a storied universe with hell beings at the base, humans and animals in the middle region, with gods and goddesses in the upper or heavenly domains. The goal within Jainism is to ascend to the Siddha Loka, a world beyond heaven and earth, where all the liberated souls dwell eternally in a state of energy, consciousness, and bliss. Although this goal utterly removes one from all worldly entanglements, the path to reach this highest attainment entails great care in regard to how one lives in relationship to all the other living beings that surround one in the earthly realm. Hence, from the aspect of practice, Jainism holds some interesting potential for ecological thinking, though its final goal transcends earthly (or earthy) concerns.

At the core of Jain faith lies five vows that dictate the daily life of Jains, laypersons, monks, and nuns. These five vows, which inspired and influenced Mahatma Gandhi, are nonviolence (ahimsa), truthfulness (satya), not stealing(asteya), sexual restraint (brahmacharya), and non-possession (aparigraha). One adheres to these vows in order to minimize harm to all possible life-forms. In Jainism, life is arranged hierarchically according to the number of senses a particular form possesses. For instance, life particles (jiva) in earth, water, fire, air, microorganisms, and plants each experience the world through the sense of touch. Worms add the sense of taste. Crawling bugs can feel, taste, and smell. Flying insects add seeing. Higher level animals, including fish and mammals, can feel, taste, smell, see, hear, and think. For observant Jains, to hurt any being results in the thickening of one's karma, obstructing advancement toward liberation. To reduce karma and prevent its further accrual, Janis avoids activities associated with violence and follows a vegetarian diet. The advanced monks and nuns will sweep their path to avoid harming insects and also work at not harming even one sensed beings such as bacteria and water.

The worldview of the Jains might be characterized as a bio cosmology. Due to their perception of the "livingness" of the world, Jains hold an affinity for the ideals of the environmental movement. The Jain vows can easily be reinterpreted in an ecological fashion. The practice of nonviolence in the Jain context fosters an attitude of respect for all life-forms. The observance of truthfulness prompts an investigation of the interrelatedness of things; a truthful person cannot easily dismiss the suffering caused by uncontrolled waste. The vow of not stealing can be used to reflect on the world's limited resources and prompt one to think of the needs of future generations. Sexual restraint might help minimize population growth. The discipline of non-possession gives one pause to think twice before indulging in the acquisition of material goods, one of the root causes of current ecological concerns. The monks and nuns, due to the heightened nature of their daily spiritual practice, leave little or no imprint on the broader ecological system. Jain people due to their care and attention to what in other philosophical traditions is none other than inert materiality, can use their experiences of applying nonviolent principles with a new, ecological intention in mind.

The Jains are particularly well-suited to reconsider their tradition in an ecological light, particularly because of their history of advocacy against meat eating and animal sacrifice, as well as their success at developing business areas that avoid overt violence. However, some challenges remain. One expression of environmentalism involves tree planting projects. Though Jaina laypeople might participate in such activities, their nuns and monks most likely would not plant trees because of the harm caused to the earth in the digging process. Another expression of environmentalism in India has been to establish forest preserves on property surrounding Jaina temple sites. However, this generally requires blocking access to prevent collection of fodder, resulting in a further impoverishment of struggling peasants. In addition to these questions of organic and social life, the extensive involvement of Janis in heavy industries in India raises issues of appropriate economic activity and environmental health. These instances demonstrate the complexity of effectively applying ecological principles in a religious context.

6.3 SIKHISM AND ENVIRONMENTAL PROTECTION:

Sikhism (Khalsa) emerged as a school of religious thought in the recent times in India. It has demonstrated through performance of its followers, the most laudable virtues of protecting and enriching the natural environment, making the most efficient use of natural resources, for man's sustained benefits in terms of food, nutrition, health and good living and developing the true spirit of partnership and sharing in community life. In Gurunanak Bani (Religious discourse), Tenn Jaga and Jagat refer to the world and convey the idea of process of creation from water, fire and air, God is the creator of these.

According to religious belief of Sikhs, there is one way, one love.

One beauty shine through air, water, and fire. One humblebee roam in the whole universe. He who understands this unity will honor.

According to Guru Nanak Dev, the immanent spirit of the God is continuously present in nature and nature is in direct and constant dependence upon His will. He is beyond the creation in the sense that while nature and human beings depend on Him.

It is tourism that there are always ups and downs in people's lives and depending on vicissitudes that they pass through. From this extremely brief view of development of '**devotion**', recurrence of casteism and rebellions against it in Hindu society appear to be one such phenomenon. What is worth noticing is that Dharma is a highly dynamic way of life, from which reform movements spring whenever there is a need to suit the changing social, economic and philosophical conditions. It may also be worth noticing that Brahmins initiated most of the rebellions against caste system. Guru Nanak is also belongs to an upper caste.

Sikhism is very concerned with the relationship between humanity and the environment. They believe that Waheguru created the world as a place where every type of plant and animal could live so that all life could have the chance to prove that it was good enough to reach **mukti** (liberation from the cycle of birth and death, reincarnation).

6.4 TEACHINGS OF GURU NANAK:

- Nature we see
- Nature we hear
- Nature we observe with awe, wonder and joy Nature in the nether regions
- Nature in the skies
- Nature in the whole creation
- Nature in species, kinds, colors
- Nature in life forms
- Nature in good deeds
- Nature in pride and in ego
- Nature in air, water, and fire
- Nature in the soil of the earth
- All nature is yours, O powerful Creator You command it, observe it and pervade within it.(Guru Granth Sahib)
- The lives of the Gurus are full of stories of their love for nature. Sikhs are forbidden to kill for the sake of killing or to eat to excess.
- In Sikh hymns Waheguru is said to be the provider of all life. There is no difference between the world of humans and the world of nature. Both of these are equally important and must be treated with respect.
- The Gurus have strongly made us aware of our responsibility towards this earth.

Guru Granth Sahib -Sikhs believe that the environment can only be preserved if the balance created by Waheguru is maintained.

6.5 SIKHISM -THE ORIGINS OF THE UNIVERSE:

Sikhism is based on the idea of the 'Oneness of Creation'. Sikhs believes the universe was made by Waheguru (God) who created the earth and all forms of life on it.

Before the creation there was no earth, no sky, no sun and no life. Only Waheguru existed until he decided to create the world. Then Waheguru created everything by a single word:

Waheguru spoke once and there was creation. Waheguru is responsible for all of creation and everything in and on the earth belongs to Waheguru. Waheguru is in charge of all life and without his hukam (will) nothing can exist, change or develop. Since creating the world Waheguru has cared for it he looks after it and protects it. Waheguru is in charge and causes the birth, life and death of everything. There is no single aspect of the earth which Waheguru does not care for. Sikhism believes that all creatures lead their lives under the rule of Waheguru.

Even creatures in rocks and stones are well provided for. Birds who fly thousands of miles away leaving their young ones behind know that they would be sustained and taught to fend for themselves by God **Guru Arjun.**

6.6 SIKHISM'S PERSPECTIVE VIEW:

It is possible to draw a parallel between the Sikh belief in the emergence of the universe from the void and the **Big Bang theory.** According to both modern science and to the Guru Granth Sahib (collection of Sikh Scriptures), there are innumerable galaxies in the universe and in each there are many solar systems containing stars and planets, all of which are in constant motion.

Sikhs believe that the universe that derived from God will ultimately be re-absorbed into God: "When the Creator became manifest, all creatures of the earth assumed various shapes. But when you draw creation within yourself, all embodied beings are absorbed in you."

Some scientists say that the expansion of the universe which followed the Big Bang will eventually be reversed and at some distant point in the future will start to contract, eventually imploding into a 'Big Crunch'.

6.7 THE ASSISI DECLARATION ON NATURE, 198T6:

6.7.1 IN THE ASSISI DECLARATION ON THE NATURE THE SIKH STATEMENT:

Since the beginning of the Sikh religion in the late fifteenth century, the faith has been built upon the message of the 'oneness of Creation'. Sikhism believes an almighty God created the universe. He himself is the creator and master of all forms of the universe, responsible for all modes of nature and all elements of the world. Sikhism firmly believes God to be the source of the birth, life and death of all things.

Sikhism teaches that the natural environment and the survival of all life forms are closely linked in the rhythm of nature. The history of the Gurus is full of stories of their love and special relationship with the natural environment-, with animals, birds, vegetation, earth, rivers, mountains and the sky. There is also a very strong vegetation tradition.

It is for this reason that in Sikhism those who kill for lust of hunting, eating or to make sacrifices are condemned. In Sikh hymns God is often referred to as the provider for all life which God loves and is loved by. God is both father and mother guarantees equality to man and woman in faith and compassion towards all beings and nature.

6.7.2 ASSISI DECLARATIONS ON NATURE:

In 1986, HRH Prince Philip, then President of the WWF International invited five leaders of five of the major religions of the world - **Buddhism Christianity, Hinduism, Islam and Judaism** - to meet to discuss how their faiths could help **save the natural world.**

The meeting took place in Assisi in Italy, because it was the birth place of St Francis, the Catholic saint of ecology. From this meeting arose key statements by the five faiths outlining their own distinctive traditions and approach to the care for nature.

6.7.3 ASSISI DECLARATION ON NATURE OF 1986 THE HINDU STATEMENT:

- The human role is not separate from nature. All objects in the universe, beings and non-beings, are pervaded by the same spiritual power.

- The human race, though at the top of the evolutionary pyramid at present, is not seen as something apart from earth and its many forms. People did not spring fully formed to dominate lesser life, but evolved out of these form and are integrally linked with them.
- **Nature is sacred** and the divine is expressed through all its forms. Reverence for life is an essential principle, as is ahimsa (non-violence).
- Nature cannot be destroyed without humanity destroying itself.
- The divine is not exterior to creation but expresses itself through natural phenomena.

6.8 JUDAISM- THE ORIGINS OF THE UNIVERSE:

Most of the world's religions have produced theories as to how the world was created and how people and animals came to be here. Usually these take the form of creation stories in the sacred books of the religions concerned.

For Judaism, the stories of the Creation are found in the in the Torah. They show how God created the world in six days and rested on the seventh. In the beginning God created the heavens and the earth.

Genesis 1:1:

After creating the earth, the sky, the seas and plants, God made birds and fish on the fifth day and animals and humans on the sixth day.

So, God created man in his own image, in the image of God he created him; male and female he created them.

Genesis 1:27:

Some Jews take this account very literally and believe that this is exactly how the world was created.

The Jewish calendar starts with the year 1 dated from the creation of the world in the book of Genesis. 1 Tishrei 1 AM (anno mundi), is equivalent to Monday, October 7, 3761 BCE. 1st January 2008 is 23 Tevet 5768.

6.9 JEWISH AND THE ENVIRONMENT PROTECTION:

Jews believe that the one God whom they worship created the heavens and earth and all forms of life in the six days of creation. Jewish teaching about caring for the environment comes from the Bible:

Then God said, 'Let us make man in our image, in our likeness, and let them rule over the fish of the sea and the birds of the air, over the livestock, over all the earth, and over all the creatures that move along the ground.' God blessed them and said to them, 'Be fruitful and increase in number; fill the earth and subdue it. Rule over the fish of the sea and the birds of the air and over every living creature that moves on the ground.'

Genesis 1:26 and 28:

Because of this passage, people see themselves as being responsible for the world which God created and they have to make their own decisions about how to do this.

6.10 JEWISH SCRIPUTER'S FESTIVALS AND ENVIRONMENT:

The Jewish Scriptures do not have a lot to say about the environment. In the Torah (major Jewish prayer) the Jews were told to rest the land once every 50 years so that it would produce more in the future (**Leviticus 25:8-11**). They were also ordered not to destroy trees when they were attacking a city:

When you lay siege to a city for a long time, fighting against it to capture it, do not destroy its trees by putting an axe to them, because you can eat their fruit. Do not cut them down. Are the trees of the field people that you should besiege them?

Deuteronomy 20:19:

Respect for trees is also shown in the annual festival of Tu B'Shevat (New Year for Trees), which takes place on fifteenth day of the Jewish month of Shevat. This has been particularly important since the founding of the State of Israel in 1948 as Israelis have tried to reclaim the desert by planting trees.

Every year, at the New Year festival of Rosh Hashanah, Jews give thanks to God for the creation of the world because, although humanity has the role of steward, the Tenakh (the collected 24 books of the Jewish Bible) shows that the earth is still God's possession: The earth is the Lord's, and everything in it, the world, and all who live in it.

Psalm 24:1:

Jews should also show respect to animals: You shall not muzzle an ox in its threshing.

Deuteronomy 25:4:

The righteous one knows [the needs of] his animal's soul.

Proverbs 12:10:

In the Assisi Declarations of1986 Rabbi Arthur Hertzberg said that:

When the whole world is in peril, when the environment is in danger of being poisoned and various species, both plant and animal are becoming extinct - it is our Jewish responsibility to put the defense of the whole of nature at the very center of our concern The encounter of God and man in nature is thus conceived in Judaism as a seamless web with man as the leader and custodian of the natural world.

****

Chapter - 7

ISLAMIC MYTHOLOGY

7.1 ISLAMIC MYTHOLOGY AND ENVIRONMENT PROTECTION:

"The life of this world is made to seem fair to those who disbelieve, and they mock those who believe. Moreover, those who keep their duty will be above them on the day of resurrection. And Allah gives to whom he pleases without measure".

In the Islamic perspective, the environmental and ecological activities were seen as a subject matter of a wonder human's effort to user in a just and peaceful society. Peace with nature based on divine ethical principles, which are immutable. According to the Islamic thought, these principles required to understand and followed by men in general so that there may not be any imbalance between men and nature.

The attitude of Islam to the environment, the sources of life, and the resources of nature based in part on prohibition of abuse, it is also based on construction and sustainable development. This integration of the development and conservation of natural resources is clear in the idea of bringing life to the land and causing it to flourish through agriculture, cultivation, and construction.

God says," It is He Who has produced you from the earth and settled you therein." The Prophet, upon him is blessings and peace, declared, "If any Muslim plants a tree or sows a field and a human, bird or animal eats from it, it shall be reckoned as charity from him." "If anyone plants a tree, neither human being nor any of **God's creatures** will eat from it without its being reckoned as charity from him. "If the day of resurrection comes upon anyone of you while he has a seedling in hand, let him plant it."

The approach of Islam toward the use and development of the earth's resources was put thus by' Ali ibn Abi-Talib, the fourth Caliph, to a man who had developed and reclaimed abandoned land: "Partake of it gladly, so long as you are a benefactor, not a despoiler; a cultivator, not a destroyer." This positive attitude involves taking measures to improve all aspects of life: health, nutrition, and the psychological and spiritual dimensions, for man's benefit and the maintenance of his welfare, as well as for the betterment of life for all future generations. If one wants to understand, the importance attached to environment,

Moreover, nature in Islam, it is necessary for him to understand the significance and meaning of Islam. Amongst the religions, tale Islam enjoys the distinction of bearing a significant name. One of the meanings of the word Islam is "to enter into peace" and Muslim is one who makes his peace with God and man. Peace with God implies neither complete submission to his will and peace with man refrain from neither evil nor injury to another but also to do good to him. Yes, whoever submits (Aslama) himself entirely to Allah and he is the doer of goods to others, he has his reward from Lord and there is no fear for such, nor shall they grieve. It is to be noted that with regard to the environment the Holy Quran refers to the element, forces and law of nature their functions and utility to man. The Quran ordains in the following terms. Moreover, my mercy encompasses all things.

7.2 ISLAMISM AND ENVIRONMENT:

Although human beings are seen as the most intelligent life form on earth, they are responsible for almost all the damage done to the planet. If we imagined the earth is aged 46, all the damage done has taken place in the last 60 seconds of the earth's life.

The Qur'an says that Allah (God) is the Creator of the world. Human beings are on the world as trustees or 'vice-regents' - they are told to look after the world for Allah and for the future:

The Earth is green and beautiful, and Allah has appointed you his stewards over it. The whole earth has been created a place of worship, pure and clean. Whoever plants a tree and diligently looks after it until it matures, and bears fruit is rewarded. If a Muslim plant a tree or sows a field and humans and beasts and birds eat from it, all of it is love on his part.

Hadith:

In the Qur'an, Muslims are instructed to look after the environment and not to damage it:

Devote thyself single-mindedly to the Faith, and thus follow the nature designed by Allah, the nature according to which He has fashioned mankind. There is no altering the creation of Allah.

Surah 30:30:

Muslims have to look after the earth because it is all Allah's creation and it is part of a human's duty to Allah:

Allah is - He who raised up the heavens without any pillars that you can see. Then He settled Himself on the Throne and constrained the sun and the moon to serve you; each planet pursues its course during an appointed term. He regulates it all and expounds the Signs, that you may have firm belief in the meeting with your Lord. He it is who spread out the earth and made therein firmly fixed mountains and rivers, and of fruits of every kind He has made pairs. He causes the night to cover the day. In all this, verily, are signs doers a people who reflect.

Surah 13:3-4:

Because of this passage, people see themselves as being **responsible** for the world which Allah created and they have to make their own decisions about how to do this.

7.3 ISLAMISM- THE ORIGINS OF THE UNIVERSE:

In the Quran (the Divine Book revealed to the Prophet Muhammad) there are details of the Creation:

Surely, your Lord is Allah. Who created the heavens and the earth in six periods; then he settled himself on the Throne. He makes the night cover the day, pursuing it swiftly. He has created the sun and the moon and the stars, all made subservient by his command…

He it is who sends the winds… Good land brings forth vegetation plentifully by the command of the Lord.

Surah 7:55-59:

I have created men, high and low, that they may worship Me. I desire no support from them, nor do I desire that they should feed Me. Surely it is Allah who is the Great Sustainer, the Lord of Power, and the Strong.

Surah 51:56:

There is no particular order given for the Creation and there is no suggestion as to how long the ayyam (periods of time) were.

7.4 MUSLIM'S PERSPECTIVE VIEW

Muslims would argue that science does not affect their belief in Allah's (God's) creation of the world; instead, it explains what the Qur'an does not say. An important part of being a Muslim is to strive for clear understanding; therefore, scientific explanations are welcomed as they help Muslims to have a greater understanding of Allah.

Muslims would say that the Qur'an has an account of the beginning of Creation which appears **very close to modern scientific theories:**

Do not the disbelievers realize that the heavens and earth were a solid mass, then we split them asunder, and we made from water every living thing? … He it is who created the night and the day, and the sun and the moon each gliding freely in its orbit.

Surah 21:31-34:

Because of the Muslim interest in and respect for science which helps them come to know and understand more about Allah, ideas from cosmology and evolutionary biology do not cause any problems.

7.5 THE TEACHINGS OF HOLY QURAN:

The Holy Quran also refers the rules and regulations for their proper and meaningful use and directions, not to disturb the balance between the different element and forces of nature.

According to Islam, the God has created the earth and implanted therein mountain hills and dales, valleys and slopes, rivers and springs, waterfalls and lakes, forests and the plains wherein dwell animals, birds and other living creatures of a thousand and one kinds. According to Holy Quran, all these are for the service of man, for his use and enjoyment, sustenance and development. However, men should not forget that there are other numerous living creatures that also have a right to exist and are entitled to use and enjoy.

Moreover, the human being must protect the nature and all living beings in order to contribute their existence to make the environment unique as, the nature filled with Lord, as the Lord is alone. **"Allah Malik ek hi".**

The holy Quran declares that everything is created from water. Thus, there is a significance of benefit purity of water. Allah is considered to be the owner of land and mankind is the trustee or guardian whereas other living creatures are considered to be the beneficiaries. In Islam also there is close harmony between man and nature.

The holy Quran declares that everything is created from water. Thus, there is a significance of benefit purity of water. Allah is considered to be the owner of land and mankind is the trustee or guardian whereas other living creatures are considered to be the beneficiaries. In Islam also there is close harmony between man and nature.

7.6 ACCORDING TO ISLAM:

According To Holy Quran the owner of land on this earth is God and whoever is in charge, possession or control thereof is only a trustee. The beneficiaries of nature are God's creatures. However, the Prophet has qualified this saying that whoever cultivates such barren land, which does not belong to anyone and plants it with trees; he acquires a right over it. It is open to a community, which is enjoying the shade of a tree, either to cut a fell it or to eat its fruit. It is therefore, submitted that Islam not only care for environment but also encouraged limited use of natural resources. The concept of trusteeship also finds place in Islam.

India has inherited a high culture of tolerance, non-violence. Equity and compassion for nature, animates, objects and as a part of daily life and is synthesized with religion. It is evidently clear that religious teachings, the social and political norms and economic policies treated man as a part of nature not as a modular to it. Air, water, land, animals, plants and human beings considered the creation of one superior power. The God, therefore, the fundamental ethics of behavior with each other was to live in harmony. It realized that each one of them is dependent on another. Destruction or damage to another is the destruction of self. One is complimentary to the other. Therefore, interdependence, co-operative living and close association with other components of environment are the real basis of human life. It became a sacred duty of human-being Homo sapiens to behave rationally and protect the nature if he wants to survive.

7.7 MUSLIM DECLARATIONS ON NATURE & ISLAMIC TEACHINGS:

Fig. 20; Muslim boys joining the "Greener Medina" initiative in Birmingham, 2007

The Muslim declaration on Nature, originated from Assisi Declarations on Nature created in 1986, at a meeting held in Assisi by WWF-International and stemming from an idea by HRH the Prince Philip at which five leaders of the five major world religions – Buddhism, Christianity, Hinduism, Islam and Judaism – were invited to come and discuss how their faiths could help save the natural world.

The essence of **Islamic teaching** is that the entire universe is **Allah's** creation. **Allah** makes the waters flows upon the earth, upholds the heavens, makes the rainfall and keeps the boundaries between day and night. The whole of the rich and wonderful universe belongs to **Allah**, its Maker. **Allah** created the plants and the animals in their pairs and gave them the means to multiply. Then **Allah** created humankind -a very special creation because humankind alone was created with reason and the power to think and even the means to turn against his Creator. Mankind has the potential to acquire a status higher than that of the angels or sink lower than the lowest of the beasts.

The word 'Islam' has the dual meaning of submission and peace. Humankind is special, a very particular creation of **Allah**. Still, we are Allah's creation and we can only properly understand ourselves when we recognize that our proper condition is one of submission to Allah who made us.

Islam teaches us that Allah has created us, that we will return to **Allah** for Judgment, and that we are accountable for our deeds as well as our omissions. Is the guidance of how to live today so that we can face the akhirah: it is the Message, which informs us, of what will be involved in that reckoning?

The central concept of Islam is Tawhid - the Unity of Allah. Allah is Unity and His Unity is reflected in the unity of mankind, and the unity of man and nature. His trustees are responsible for maintaining the unity of His creation, the integrity of the Earth, its flora and fauna, its wildlife and natural environment. Unity cannot be had by discord, by setting one need against another; it is maintained by balance and harmony. Therefore, Muslims say that Islam is the middle path and we will be answerable for how we have walked this path and how we have maintained balance and harmony in the whole of creations around us.

The Prophet of Islam, says that Who so ever plants a tree and diligently looks after it until it matures and bears fruit is rewarded'. And 'If a Muslim plants a tree or sows a field and men and beats and birds eat from it, all of it is a charity on his part', and again, 'The world is green and beautiful, and **Allah** has appointed as His stewards over it.' Environmental consciousness is born when such values are adopted and become an intrinsic part of our mental and physical make-up

The classical Muslim jurist, Izzard-Din Ibn Abdas-Salam, used these aspects of the Shari'ah when he formulated the bill of legal rights of animals in the thirteenth century. Similarly, numerous other jurists and scholars developed legislations to safeguard water resources, prevent over-grazing, conserve forests, limit the growth of cities, protect cultural property, and so on. Islam's environmental ethics then are not limited to metaphysical notions; they provide a practical guide as well.

Muslims need to turn to this nexus of values, this way of understanding themselves and their environment. The notions of unity, trusteeship and accountability should not be reduced to matters of personal piety; they must guide all aspects of their life and work. Shari'ah should not be relegated just to issues of crime and punishment; it must also become the vanguard for environmental legislation.

Islam is a complete way of life, by which it is meant that our ethical system provides the bearings for all our actions. Yet our actions often undermine the very values we cherish. Often while working as scientists or technologists, economists or politicians, we act contrary to the environmental dictates of Islam. We must imbibe these values into our very being. We must judge our actions by them. They furnish us with a worldview, which enables us to ask environmentally appropriate questions, to draw up the right balance sheet of possibilities, and to properly weigh the environmental costs and benefits of what we, want, what we can do within the ethical boundaries established by **Allah**, without violating the rights of His other creations.

7.7.1 THE ASSISI DECLARATIONS ON NATURE 1986:

In 1986, HRH Prince Philip, then President of the WWF International invited five leaders of five of the major religions of the world - **Buddhism, Christianity, Hinduism, Islam and Judaism** - to meet to discuss how their faiths could help **save the natural world.**

The meeting took place in Assisi in Italy, because it was the birthplace of St Francis, the Catholic saint of ecology. From this meeting arose key statements by the five faiths outlining their own distinctive traditions and approach to the care for nature.

In the Assisi Declarations on Nature the Muslim statement was:

- The central concept of Islam is Tawhid or the Unity of God. Allah is Unity; and His Unity is also reflected in the unity of mankind, and the unity of man and nature. His trustees are responsible for maintaining the unity of His creation, the integrity of the Earth, its flora and fauna, its wildlife and natural environment. Unity cannot be had by discord, by setting one need against another or letting one end predominate over another; it is maintained by balance and harmony. There Muslims say that Islam is the middle path, and we will be answerable for how we have walked this path, how we have maintained balance and harmony in the whole of creation around us.
- So, unity, trusteeship, and accountability, that is Tawhid, Khalifah and Akhirah, the three central concepts of Islam, are also the pillars of the environmental ethics of Islam. They constitute the basic values taught by the Qur'an. It is these values which led Muhammad, the Prophet of Islam, to say: 'whoever plants a tree and diligently looks after it until it matures, and bears fruit is rewarded.'
- For all these reasons Muslims see themselves as having a responsibility towards the world and the environment, all of which are the creations of Allah.
- Unlike many other religions, Muslims do not have any specific festivals in which they give thanks for the harvest or the world. Instead, they give thanks to Allah regularly for his creation.
- To separate Islam from other religions, the Islamic year is only 354 days, this means that the months and festivals happen at a different time each year and so there is no particular festival which falls during a period of harvest.

7.8 TODAY'S SITUTATION:

Today, the situation is just the other way round. We call those Communities shall adhere to the old principles. Most of these communities have annihilated. It is tragic that the new world has created on the graves of the old world: the old world, which lived in harmony with nature.

Therefore, it is a well-established fact that in ancient India the people had a deeper relationship with plants and trees. The contribution of men to the life of plants and trees in turn was equally important. They tend to form more relationship that is intimate. Hence, the primitive people of India always treated the plants and trees as a part of their families. We should not deviate from the path of our ancestors regarding the environment protection.

****

Chapter – 8

CHRISTIANITY

8.1. Christian religion and Environment: 8.1.1 Christianity: beliefs about creation and evolution, 8.2 Different views Of Christians and teachings of the churches: a) Teachings of the churches, 8.2.1 Scientific ideas Of Christians, 8.3 Christianity & Cosmology, 8.4 Principle of Sustained Order and Purpose, 8.5. Religious Partnerships in Action, 8.6 All Creation Matters: a) Our Response, 8.7 Reverences for Creation, 8.8. Principles and Practice of a Christian Environmental Ethic: Conclusions.

8.1 CHRISTIAN RELIGION AND ENVIRONMENT:

Religions provide basic interpretive stories of who we are, what nature is, where we have come from, and where we are going. This comprises a worldview of a society. Religions also suggest how we should treat other humans and how we should relate to nature. Religions thus generate worldviews and ethics, which underlie fundamental attitudes and values of different cultures and societies. Christianity has a long historical tradition of reflection on nature and human responsibility. Green Christians point out that the biblical emphasis is on stewardship, not ownership--that the earth remains the Lord's (Psalms 24:1) and does not belong to its human inhabitants.

The strategy of Christian stewardship frames environmental issues around faithful response to God's invitation and command. By appropriating the biblical trope of stewardship, this strategy organizes concern for environmental problems around obligatory service to the Creator, who entrusts to humans measured responsibilities for creation.

The stewardship strategy thus makes environmental issues significant in light of God's attitude toward human agents, situating environmental practices wholly within the exchange between God and humanity. God's action claims, guides, and measures right human action with regard to other creatures. Environmental responsibilities therefore matter for Christian moral experience with respect to God's giving and forgiving—the grace of providence and the grace of redemption. "The principle of stewardship is closely linked to the concept of grace: everything comes from God as a gift and is to be administered faithfully on his behalf."

Patriarch of orthodox Christianity's mother church, recently made declaration that environmental harm is sinful. Public attention has drawn to the energy by bringing faith in people to defense of creation. Many Christians and Jews, their faith calls on them to care for the earth's bounty; its air, waters, land all plant and animal species.

The Bible teaches that when we put our faith and trust in Jesus Christ, He will lead us to an eternal heavenly home prepared by God. However, until we are called to live forever with God in our heavenly homes, we must live within the physical homes God has provided for us.

These physical homes include the entire planet earth, the various natural environments found on the planet, our towns and cities, and the houses or apartments where we lay our heads down at night to sleep. We all live on the same planet and are ultimately dependent on the natural fruits of the earth for life-support, everyone has a stake in how elements of nature and natural systems are used and managed. When a specific natural resource or environmental issue or problem arises, individuals and groups often disagree on the appropriate course of action to resolve the issue or problem. At the core of these disagreements are different values and beliefs related to nature itself, and the use and management of nature by people. A growing number of scholars in the humanities, social sciences and physical and biological sciences are emphasizing that environmental issues and problems are fundamentally interrelated with ethical issues and problems (Daly; Means; Santmire; Schaeffer; Stewart; Van Dyke et al; White). Consequently, we are hearing more voices saying that in order to solve environmental issues and problems, people need to develop and follow an appropriate "moral basis" for dealing with nature. This recognizes a basic tenant of human behavior taught in the Bible: true change starts from within a person's heart, mind, spirit, and works outward as reflected by attitudes and actions. In all areas of our lives, the substance of our inner faith determines the living out or practice of our faith.

In 1989, Pope John Paul 2 warned that materialistic greed is contrary to the "mutual interdependence" that is the "**order of creation**".

Catholic Christians should have a deep reverence and a deep sense of awe towards God's creation. This deep reverence and sense of awe at creation should stir us to care about our environment and to conserve our resources.

8.1.1 CHRISTIANITY- BELIEFS ABOUT CREATION AND EVOLUTION:

Many of the world's religions have ideas and beliefs about the origin of the universe, including people and animals. Usually these take the form of creation accounts in the sacred books of the religions concerned.

The origins of the universe:

Genesis 1:1-2:4a:
This account tells how **God created the world in six days and rested on the seventh**. In the beginning God created the heavens and the earth.

Genesis 1:1:
After creating the earth, the sky, the seas and plants, **God made birds and fish on the fifth day and animals and humans on the sixth day**. So God created man in his own image, in the image of God he created him; male and female he created them. (Genesis 1.27)

Genesis 1-2:
God created the universe out of nothing and continues to sustain all creation. Also suggests that the task of human beings is to reflect God's creative love and their covenant relationships with God, by caring for the earth as good stewards and as faithful gardeners.

Genesis: 1:27-31
God created humanity in his image; in the divine image, he created him; male and female he created them. God blessed them, saying: "Be fertile and multiply; fill the earth and cultivate it. Exercise stewardship over the fish of the sea, the birds of the air, and all the living things that move on the earth." God also said: "See, I give you every seed-bearing plant all over the earth and every tree that has seed-bearing fruit on it to be your food; and to all the animals of the land, all the birds of the air, and all the living creatures that crawl on the ground, I give all the green plants for food." Therefore, it happened. God looked at everything he had made, and he found it very good.

Genesis: 9:3-4

Every creature that is alive shall be yours to eat; I give them all to you as I did the green plants. Only flesh with its lifeblood still in it you shall not eat.

In the Biblical narrative, it is only after the great flood that humanity is given the right to eat animal flesh. Humanity is portrayed as originally vegetarian and remained vegetarian for some time after the Fall. In the mystical theology and spirituality of the desert mothers and fathers, saints are often portrayed conversing with animals and living in harmony with all creation. The prophet Isaiah even for tells a day when the lion and the lamb will lie together in peace, and one can presume that humanity will live at peace with the animals in these days as well. In monastic traditions, many Christians continued to embrace vegetarianism for centuries. Unfortunately, this spirituality has been largely lost in the West.

It is interesting to note that even when the right to animal flesh is given in the Biblical narrative, we are not to take the blood of the animals, which is a symbol of life.

Genesis 2:4b-25:

Fig. 21: Adam and Eve leaving Eden

This is a much earlier account. It describes how the Lord God first of all created a man by taking some soil from the ground and breathing life into him.

God placed the man in a garden in Eden, and made beautiful trees grow there. God said to the man:

You may eat the fruit of any tree in the garden, except the tree that gives knowledge of what is good and what is bad. You must not eat the fruit of that tree; if you do you will die that same day.

Genesis 2: 16-17:
The Lord God took soil and formed the animals and birds; the man named them, but none was a suitable companion for him. The Lord God put the man into a deep sleep, and while he slept, he took one of the man's ribs and formed a woman out of it.

Genesis 2:15:
Man was to work the Garden of Eden and care for it He was to use but not abuse it. In today's language his use was to be sustainable.

8.2 DIFFERENT VIEWS OF CHRISTIANS AND TEACHINGS OF THE CHURCHES:

There is a variety of interpretations of the biblical accounts of creation among Christians today.

Most believe that God brought the universe into being from nothing (ex nihilo); some believe that it was created from matter that already existed (ex material).

Some Christians take the biblical accounts of creation literally, believing that they describe exactly how the universe and human beings were created.

Other Christians regard these accounts as more like parables or symbolic accounts that tell (in story form) the profound truth that God brought the universe and all that is in it into being and sustains his creation. These Christians might look to science to help them understand how God did this.

a) TEACHINGS OF THE CHURCHES:

Environmental issues and climate change in particular, have begun to appear in the teachings of various churches over the past thirty years. For example, the World Council of Churches (1997) made a statement about the duties of mankind with respect to the environment at the meeting for the ratification of the Kyoto treaty.

At one extreme, the Roman Catholic Church takes a progressive view on the environment. The catechism, updated in 1993, species that mankind, although distinct from the animals, has "solidarity" with them by virtue of sharing the same creator (Vat-ican, 1993, paragraphs 337-344). Furthermore an appeal to virtue is made in opposition to unnecessary animal cruelty (paragraphs 2418, 2457). The US catholic bishops support calls from the scientific community for action on climate change (United States Conference of Catholic Bishops, 2001).

At the other extreme, a recent call to action by some US evangelical leaders was op-posed by some well know evangelists and a spokesman for the Southern Baptist Convention 3(Hagerty, 2006). The web site of the Baptist World Alliance (2006) does not have a position document on the environment. The Baptist Union of Great Britain (2006) does have such a document, but the position is one of dominion tempered by stewardship.

The fundamentalist wing of the evangelical movement is much more wary of science, especially evolutionary biology, and supports this position by emphasizing Genesis 1-2 over the rest of scriptures.

8.2.1 SCIENTIFIC IDEAS OF CHRISTIANS:

For many Christians there isn't a conflict between the religious ideas about creation expressed in Genesis and the findings of science. **Professor John Polkinghorne** is both a scientist and a priest in the Church of England; he says:

Genesis is not there to give short, technical answers about how the universe began. It gives us the big answer that things exist because of God's will. One can perfectly well believe in the Big Bang, but believe in it as the will of God the creator.

8.3 CHRISTIANITY & COSMOLOGY:

Cosmology is the study of the universe, and humanity's place in it.

One of the theories put forward by cosmologists is the **Big Bang theory.** This suggests that about 15 billion years ago there was a massive explosion. This was the point at which all matter in the universe began; space and time began then too. Over time the universe that we know, and human and animal life, emerged. This theory has been generally accepted by scientists as being the best one. Scientists have to explain the origins of the universe. If this theory is true, then it could mean that the universe 'just happened' and that it did not emerge because of the activity of a creator God.

Many Christians have no problem in accepting the Big Bang theory. They see the cosmologists helping them to understand how God brought the world into being - the Big Bang could have been the mechanism God used. And there is nothing in the theory itself which proves that there is no such being as God.

Christian teaching about caring for the environment comes from the Bible:

Then God said, 'Let us make man in our image, in our likeness, and let them rule over the fish of the sea and the birds of the air, over the livestock, over all the earth, and over all the creatures that move along the ground.'... God blessed them and said to them, 'Be fruitful and increase in number; fill the earth and subdue it. Rule over the fish of the sea and the birds of the air and over every living creature that moves on the ground.'

Christians say in the Apostles' Creed:

I believe in one God, the Father, the almighty, maker of heaven and earth.

8.4 PRINCIPLES OF SUSTAINED ORDER AND PURPOSE:

The Principle of Sustained Order and Purpose implies that God originally created all elements of nature to fit and function together in an orderly fashion within interrelated systems to meet certain ongoing purposes. God's direct involvement in natural systems did not end after the original creation period described in Genesis 1. The triune God continues to hold together or sustain the functioning of nature, accomplishing His intended order and purpose of all nonliving and living elements of nature and natural systems.

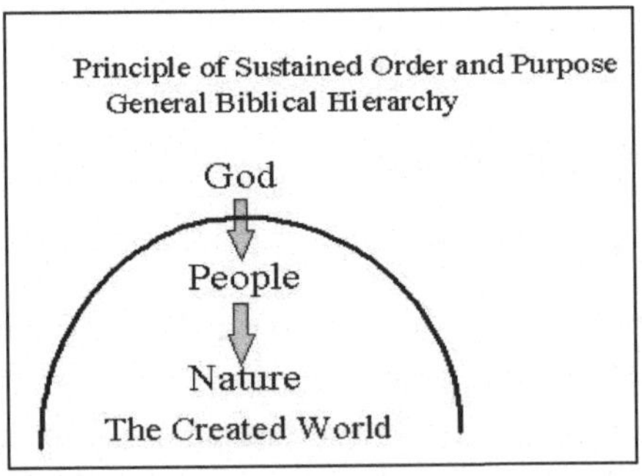

Fig: 22Principle of Sustained Order and Purpose – General Biblical Hierarchy

Above figure, shows a fundamental separation between God and his creation including people. God is above people and nature and both people and elements of nature such as plants and animals must interact and live together within the same created world governed by God's ways and plans. Thus, people share a common heritage and bond with plants, animals and other elements of nature as fellow creations of God. People, like plants and animals, must also cope with living in a physical world and universe created and controlled by God.

The diagram also illustrates that within the physical world and universe, people are above nature. People are above nature by the grace and will of God only - not by our own power and ingenuity. God created people in His image to exercise Godly dominion over nature. Godly dominion over nature means that people act as stewards or caretakers of nature who are ultimately responsible to God for their use and management of nature.

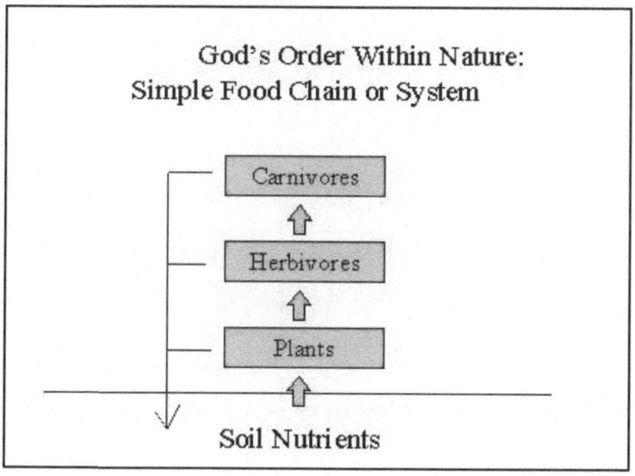

Fig:23God's Order within Nature Simple Food Chain or System

In Fig 23, living plants take nutrients from the soil. Herbivores such as rabbits or deer eat plants for food. Carnivores such as mountain lions eat other animals for food. When plants and animals die, microorganisms in the environment decompose the plant and animal body material into basic chemicals that go back into the soil. These chemicals then taken up by plants for nutrients completing the cycling of life-supporting chemicals through the environment.

People are also dependent on the food chain and chemical cycling systems illustrated in Fig 22. The linkages and interrelationships between people and elements of nature and natural systems are illustrated at a broader scale in Fig 23.

Fig 23 illustrates the planet earth home God has provided for all of us, and the global interrelation ship between people and nature.

The scientific study of natural life-support systems falls under the realm of ecology. The word ecology is derived from the Greek root words, “eco” meaning “house” and “logy” meaning “study”. The word ecology can therefore be literally interpreted to mean “house study” or the “study of the house”. The “house” being referred to here is the planet earth and its natural systems. Before describing how the earth’s natural systems provide life-support, consider the artificial life-support systems that people build into the various dwellings we call home at a small scale.

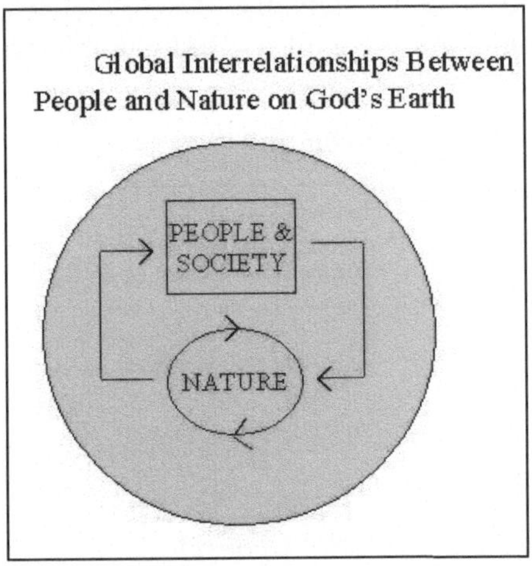

Fig 24: Global Interrelationships between People and Nature on God’s Earth

The scientific study of natural life-support systems falls under the realm of ecology. The word ecology derived from the Greek word, “eco” meaning “house” and “logo” means “study”. The word ecology literally means “house study” or the “study of the house”. The “house” being referred to here is the planet earth and its natural systems. Before describing how the earth’s natural systems provide life-support, consider the artificial life-support systems that people build into the various dwellings we call home at a small scale.

Actually, the physical dwellings that people construct are with certain life-support systems. These artificial life-support systems include air circulation systems to regulate oxygen (O2) and carbon dioxide (CO2) levels so that indoor air to breathe. And the water systems to provide safe and secure drinking heating and cooling systems to regulate indoor temperatures at healthy levels; and waste disposal systems that help to prevent illness by safely and regularly removing potential germ-producing human wastes and garbage.

On the Earth's planet the forests, deserts, oceans, lakes and rivers created by God with natural life-support systems. God built several major chemical cycles into our planet earth home. Each of these cycles helps to provide all that needed to support life on earth. For example, the carbon and oxygen cycle helps to provide breathable air and regulate global temperatures at livable levels. The hydrologic cycle helps to provide water to drink and for a multitude of other purposes.

The different chemical cycles also contribute to the provision of mineral resources such as coal, oil and natural gas that we use as fuel for transportation, electricity, and heating. These cycles also support renewable resources such as trees and fish and wildlife. We use trees for consumptive uses as lumber, and to support non-consumptive uses such as recreation and aesthetic enjoyment. We use fish and wildlife for consumptive uses such as harvesting ocean fish for food, and hunting of wildlife on public and private lands. We also use fish and wildlife for non-consumptive recreational uses and aesthetic enjoyment such as wildlife observation and photography (Barrett and Bergstrom).

When people use elements of nature for commercial production and consumption, and even recreational and aesthetic enjoyment, some level of waste-by products enter the environment. Smoke stakes into the air and effluent discharge pipes into rivers are obvious evidence of these waste by-products. When people use a forest or park for recreation, waste by-products are emitted into the air from automobiles, and motorboats. Solid wastes in the form of litter are also often left behind.

God has built waste assimilation and treatment capabilities into natural systems. For example, scientists have documented the natural ability of wetlands to filter chemicals out of water that are potentially harmful to human health. However, excessive use of a particular natural system such as a wetland area by people for waste by-product disposal may threaten the continued ability of that natural system to assimilate and treat wastes.

The Principle of Sustained Order and Purpose has emphasized that God created people and nature with order and purpose. In God's ordering people is over nature meaning that people may take from nature to meet their needs. However, God also expects people to give back to nature, as one of God's intended purposes for people is to act as responsible caretakers of nature.

8.5 RELIGIOUS PARTNERSHIPS IN ACTION:

An ecumenical group, the National Religious Partnership for the environment founded in 1993 in order to educate Christians and Jews about the role of humanity's duty.

Evangelical environment network collaborates in publication of a quarterly magazine, creation care caring for the environment from a Biblical Perspective. Evangelical environment network made declaration on the "care of creations" in 1994.

Catholics took part to restore coastal; wetlands in LOUISIANA. The Red wood Rabbis have worked in Northern California to stop the clear cutting of old growth forests.

The Christian environmental association conducts research and education at a centre in Belize, acquires endangered lands through its Eden conservancy and offers an academic study on environmental degradation, resource depletion and population growth.

There are six key principles that underlie Christian beliefs about ecology and the environment. These principals have informed the thought, writings and actions of many famous Christians across the centuries, including Augustine of Hippo, Hildegard of Bingen, Irenaeus, John Bunyan, Julian or Norwich and Teilhard de Chardin.

These six are:

- The goods of the earth are to be shared by all.
- It is important to live in a safe and life-giving environment.
- The diversity of life has inherent value because it testifies to the grandeur and glory of God the Creator.
- Aesthetic and prayerful appreciation of the beauty of the universe is a classic path to knowledge and love of God.
- Attempts at resolving environmental abuses (such as pollution, acid rain) must not ignore the poor, who share the human right to authentic development.

- A new spirit of solidarity among all nations is needed to resolve global environmental issues

8.6 ALL CREATION MATTERS:

Religious leader say that protecting the environment goes to the "**heart of living the faith**" and environmental destruction is a sign of lost in moral bearings. The Genesis story of creation, illustrated the central importance of biological diversity and interdependence in God's plan. Creation is a place of 'shalom' of flourishing fitness.

Christian and Jewish scholars have delved deeply into their heritage to illuminate the Biblical concepts that support caring for the creation. "Because of God's wise and orderly creative activity, the diverse kinds of creatures fit together into a harmonious whole."O Lord, how manifold is your works! In wisdom, you have made them all. The earth is full of your possessions."

Much attention has given to God's command that in Genesis, people are given dominion over all life. That pronouncement, Dr. Bouma-Prediger wrote, is not a license for man to do as he pleases with God's creation, but to take responsible care of it.

Genesis 2:15 calls on man to till keep the Earth. Bouma-Prediger wrote that, when examined in the original Hebrew, this passage "speaks to our task to serve (Abad) and protect (shamar) the garden that is the earth."

Perhaps the most telling illustration is the story of the great flood, when God ordered Noah to gather one male and one female of every type of living creature to begin life again after the deluge. Afterward, extinguish God made a covenant that never again would life. Importantly, as is written in Genesis, that covenant made with "every living creature."

God entrusted His creation to Adam and Eve–and consequently to all of us. The Lord of all creation gave us the awesome responsibility to care for the created world, both for ourselves and for generations to come. Therefore, the world is not a hostile environment from which we seek refuge. Rather, God's people have always considered creation as an object of praise, as it reflects the goodness and might of our heavenly Father.

This brief biblical overview helps us to understand the Church's positive, balanced approach to the environment. We understand our privileged place in creation and the right to use the created world for our benefit. Yet, we also understand that the seventh commandment puts appropriate limits on our use of the world's resources and summons us to approach the environment with profound respect (see Catechism, no. 2415). Our stewardship and "dominion" cannot be separated from our moral responsibilities toward the created world and our neighbors, including future generations (see Catechism, no. 2456).

Psalm 104, revealed that all creatures are testament to God's unsurpassed power.

Mat 6:26-27: Turn to the New Testament and God still cares about his creatures We therefore have a continuous witness about the importance of the environment from Adam to Noah to Moses to Jesus.

Rom 8:19-22: The Earth has a future, even after Jesus' return. It will be renewed and will be our eternal home (2 Pet 3:13).Although the Earth will ultimately be renewed, the present destruction of the environment cannot be ignored. In fact, in Rev 8:7-11 it seems to be a means of judgment. (The imagery is symbolic, but are we seeing a fulfillment of this now as the Earth heats up, as the oceans become acidified, and as our rivers become polluted and saline.

A) OUR RESPONSE:

We should acknowledge that the Bible makes plain our responsibility to care for the environment, a responsibility we have neglected. We should also acknowledge that God speaks to us, not just through his word, but also through his creation (Psa 19:1-4, Rom 1:20, Mat 6:28-29).

As individual believers, and as churches, we need to repent of our environmental carelessness, and of our sometimes-willful ignorance. Although we may have to live with some of the consequences of our past environmental failings, that humbly acknowledge these to God, the healing of the land will begin (2 Chr 7:14).

We should accept our duty of stewardship over the environment (Gen 1:26-28). As green groups have been telling us for decades, this involves acting locally and thinking globally.

Acting locally involves reasonable measures to minimize the harm we do to the environment personally.

Thinking globally means acknowledging the role of government in those areas that are properly its concern. We should "give to Caesar what is Caesar's" (Mat 22:15-22), and cooperate with government in seeking the common good (Rom 13:1-7). These scriptures refer specifically to the right of governments to levy taxes, and their duty to preserve law and order. I would argue that protecting the environment is also very much the business of government, both at the national level and in appropriate international agreements. There is nothing we have more in common than the air we breathe, the water we drink, and the climate all God's creatures and we live in. Because these things cross the boundaries between nations, our response must be local, national, and global.

Our legitimate concern for the environment should not distract us from our primary focus, which is the extension of the Kingdom of God (Mat 6:19-21). Nevertheless, care for the environment is part of responsible living through which we honour God and witness to the world (Mat 5:16).

8.7 REVERENCES FOR CREATION:

Creation itself is a revelation of the unsurpassed glory of God's works. Nature reveals the future perfection promised by God. Reverence for creation powerfully expressed in Jewish thoughts. The Jewish laws of rescue can be read as commandments to save the environment, for the sake of saving humanity, The earth will undoubtedly survive our degradation and will continue to swarm with life, but humankind may be extinguished and this stage of God's experiment on the earth.

The challenge a head is the common challenge of science and religion together, to discover and implement the means of assuring to physical survival of humanity on earth, to discover and implement the means of assuring the spiritual survival of more humble and more modest humanity on this God's earth.

Moses 6:63: Jesus Christ created the earth and heaven under the direction of Heavenly Father. Everywhere you look you can see all that they created for you. The Sun, Stars, Seas, Animals, Trees, Flowers, Fruits, Vegetables, and all that shows that you have a Heavenly Father and a Savior who loves you. It pleased them to create the earth and all the things upon it to bless you and help you be happy.

Stewardship and reverence for creation are central tenets of all faiths on Earth. The extraordinary delicacy of Nature's balance is becoming increasingly apparent, even as human actions inflict ever larger, more dangerous and potentially irreversible changes on the indivisible web of atmosphere, earth, ocean and life that is creation. Today our faiths stand united in their call to care for the Earth, and to protect the poor and the suffering. Strong action on climate change is imperative by the principles and traditions of our faiths and the collective compassion, wisdom and leadership of humanity.

It is recognized that the science of climate change, and we call for global leaders to adopt strong, binding, science-based targets for the reduction of greenhouse gases in order to avert the worst dangers of a climate crisis. We urge the nations of earth to ensure that those who will suffer under climate-induced changes such as more severe storms, floods, droughts and rising seas, be aided to adapt, survive and equitably prosper.

It has recognized that the climate change is not merely an economic or technical problem, but rather at its core is a moral, spiritual and cultural one. Therefore, pledge to join to teach and guide the people who follow the call of our faiths. One must all learn to live together within the shared limits of our planet. Mitigating climate change can stimulate economic sustainable, protect our planet, lift up the poor, and unite to a common cause people threatened by a common danger. Assisting vulnerable communities and species to survive and adapt to climate change fulfills our calling to wisdom, mercy, and the highest of human moral and ethical values. We commit ourselves to action – to changing our habits, our choices, and the way we see the world – to learning and teaching our families, friends, and faiths – to conserving the limited resources of our home, planet Earth, and preserving the climate conditions upon which life depends.

"To commit a crime against the natural world is a sin". "The Earth is the Lord's and all its fullness, the world those who dwell there in" (Psalm 24:1).

"Your land must not be sold on a permanent basis because you do not own it", it belongs to God and you are like foreigners who are allowed to make use of it (Leviticus 25:23).

Rev 11:18. "Destroy those who destroy the earth."

In Rev 11:18 we find an interesting plea by the angels to God in his role as final judge. They say "the time has come to destroy those who destroy the earth."

8.8 PRINCIPLES AND PRACTICE OF A CHRISTIAN ENVIRONMENTAL ETHIC: CONCLUSIONS:

Today we are facing with many natural resource and environmental issues and problems. There issues and problems are related to managing nature and the natural resources provided by nature to provide food for eating, paper for writing, lumber for construction, and areas for people to participate in outdoor recreation and experience aesthetic enjoyment of nature. There are issues and problems related to protecting nature from many source of degradation or damage by people (Dewitt). If nature is degraded or damaged by people (or even by itself), there are issues and problems related to how to go about repairing or mitigating the environmental damage.

Christians are in a unique position to offer thoughtful solutions to the natural resource and environmental problems and issues we face in the world today. There is growing recognition on the part of people from a variety of professional and personal backgrounds that effective, long-term solutions to natural resource and environmental problems and issues requires an appropriate moral basis for action. God's word found in the Holy Bible provides this moral basis in the form of a Christian environmental ethic that results in responsible and caring stewardship of all of God's creation.

The Christian environmental ethics are the Principle of Creation Value, the Principle of Sustained Order and Purpose, and the Principle of Universal Corruption and Redemption. To practice effective Christian environmental stewardship, one must work on increasing knowledge of these principles.

Once we have become a new creation or person in Christ, our minds and thinking can be renewed in many areas of our lives. In the area of environmental stewardship, a deep, personal understanding of the way God loves and sustains all of His creation gives us a new and proper perspective of the temporal and eternal value and purposes of nature. This understanding, when taken to heart, transforms how we view and carry out our God-given role as caretakers of nature.

Christian caretakers of nature may be farmers, foresters, or anglers who manage and harvest the land and waters of the earth in a productive and sustainable manner. They may be professional biologists, botanists, ecologists or other environmental scientists who study nature and develop scientific solutions to problems and challenges related to managing specific parts of nature or entire natural systems. They may be toxicologists or other human health specialist who study the effects of environmental pollutants on people in order to develop waste gg management and pollution control strategies that protect and maintain our health and quality of life.

Christian caretakers of nature may be professional economists, sociologists, or political scientists who study economic and social systems in order to help solve problems and challenges related people's use of natural resources and impacts on the environment. There may also be philosophers or theologians who help us to understand the proper Biblical perspectives on the worth and purposes of people and nature. Professors at colleges and universities and teachers at secondary schools can also be Christian caretakers of nature through teaching, research and public service activities that focus on providing needed information and equipping other to meet natural resource and environmental problems and challenges now and in the future in a Christian manner.

The fact of the matter is that every Christian can and should be a Christian caretaker of nature no matter what his or her vocation or position in life happens to be. The Christian steward of nature first recognizes that nature, like everything else in heaven and earth, was created by God, belongs to God, and valued by God for itself. The Christian steward helps to utilize nature as God intended in the service of both God and people. When making use of nature, the Christian steward recognizes that he or she has a responsibility to manage or take care of nature in a way that is not wasteful or destructive of the original functions of nature designed by God.

The Christian steward respects plants, animals and other elements of nature in their created order out of respect for the triune God - Father, Son and Holy Spirit who created and continues to sustain the entire earth and universe. The Christian steward also respects and values nature because he or she knows that both people and nature will share in redemption and renewal in the new eternal heaven and earth. Respecting and valuing nature never makes nature the object of a Christian steward's worship. Rather, credit and honor and worship always goes to the Creator of nature and not nature itself in the same way that credit and honor for a magnificent piece of art work does not go to the art work itself, but to the artist who created it.

****

Chapter- 9

ENVIRONMENTAL DISASTERS & PREDICTIONS

9.0 INTRODUCTION:

Despite the fact that humans have made tremendous progress in various aspects in terms of technological growths, yet there is one area where they have not been able to surpass and that is the supremacy of Nature. Nature has always proved much more powerful than the human race, even though there have been lot of technological and scientific advancements and achievements. In spite of development in weather forecast techniques, disasters at many times cannot be prevented. In today's age, the natural calamities in the form of floods, tsunamis, famines, cyclones, earthquakes are mainly due to global warming. Time and again, we have seen and read about many natural disasters occurring in the country and outside, which have caused a great havoc in the society, killing thousands of people and destroying lives and properties. Most dangerous natural disasters occurring in the history of India over the years are mentioned briefly.

9.1 MADHAV DHANANJAYA GADGIL:

Madhav Dhananjaya Gadgil was born in 1942.He received Padma Bhushan award. Madhav Dhananjaya Gadgil is an Indian ecologist, academic, writer, columnist and the founder of the Centre for Ecological Sciences, a research forum under the aegis of the Indian Institute of Science.

The Western Ghats Ecology Expert Panel, also known as the Gadgil Commission after its chairman Madhav Gadgil, was an environmental research commission appointed by the Ministry of Environment and Forests of India.

The Gadgil Committee (formed by the Central Government headed by Prof. Madhav Gadgil), which is formally known as Western Ghats Ecology Expert Panel (WGEEP), submitted its report to concerned authorities in August 2011. In the report, the committee had predicted a flood situation at that point in time, urging the government to take steps to protect the Western Ghats. But all the governments rejected the report claiming it is "too environment-friendly". Experts have contradicted the claims and said that the reason is also unplanned development, cutting of trees and illegal forest land acquisition at the Western Ghats.

9.1.1 KEY FINDINGS OF THE REPORT:

1. The Western Ghats Ecology Expert Panel (WGEEP) designated the entire Western Ghats as an Ecologically Sensitive Area (ESA). It divided the area into three zones depending on ecological vulnerability: Ecologically Sensitive Zone 1 (ESZ1), Ecologically Sensitive Zone 2 (ESZ2) and Ecologically Sensitive Zone 3 (ESZ3), and the assignment was done at the Taluka level.
2. It recommended that no new dams based on large-scale storage be permitted in Ecologically Sensitive Zone 1 as defined by the panel. This included a suggestion to not give clearance to the Athirappilly and Gundia hydel projects.
3. For all settlements and built areas/ to be developed areas, certain types of areas would be no-go areas, including watercourses, water bodies, special habitats, geological formations, biodiversity-rich areas, and sacred groves. Special Economic Zones should not be permitted. New hill stations should not be allowed and public lands should not be converted to private lands.

4. A building code should be evolved which includes inter-alia eco-friendly building material and construction methods, minimizing the use of steel, cement, and sand, providing water harvesting methods, non-conventional energy and waste treatment. The application or detailing of the framework would be done by local authorities to suit local conditions.
5. Certain practices recognized as the best construction/development ones such as topsoil conservation, trees conservation, etc. should be followed as per the guidelines of Green Building certifications of Eco Housing and GRIHA. Any other appropriate codes are also to be encouraged. Certain activities such as filling of marshes/ wetlands, the introduction of alien invasive species are not permitted. The area that may be saved is to be restricted; paving of ground areas may be done in such a manner that there is no change in the run-off/permeability of the plot overall before and after paving (if some area is paved, the recharge from other areas will have to be enhanced).
6. Local authorities should be made responsible for developing regional systems for handling hazardous, toxic, biomedical wastes as well as recyclable materials.
7. Promote organic agricultural practices; discourage cultivation of annual crops on slopes exceeding 30%, where perennial crops should be promoted; introduce incentive payments for sequestration of carbon in soils, introduce incentive payments for maintenance of select traditional cultivars, encourage participatory breeding programs to improve the productivity of traditional cultivars; encourage precision in agricultural practices.
8. Forest Rights Act to be implemented in its true spirit by reaching out to people to facilitate their claims, Community Forest Resource provisions under FRA to replace all current Joint Forest Management programs.
9. No new licenses to be given for mining. Where mining exists, it should be phased out in 5 years, by 2016. Detailed plans for environmental and social rehabilitation of mines are to be closed. Illegal mining should also to be stopped immediately.
10. Educate the energy consumer about the environmental and social impacts of energy production and the need for reducing luxury demand. Encourage demand-side management; enhanced energy efficiency across sectors. Launch smart campaigns as key components of demand-side management, focusing on smart grids, smart buildings, smart power, smart logistics and smart motors. Promote decentralized electricity and use of solar power.

9.2 KERALA FLOODS (2018):

The Ecologist Madhav Gadgil, founder of the Centre for Ecological Sciences at the Indian Institute of Science, Bangalore, has described the floods in Kerala as a man-made disaster; a reaction to the illegal excavations, stone quarrying done over a decade. Most of the areas affected by this monsoon were once classified as ecologically-sensitive zones by the Western Ghats Ecology Expert Panel, also known as the Gadgil Committee, formed in 2010 the Centre. Gadgil said, "Irresponsible environmental policy is to be blamed for the recent floods and landslides in Kerala.

Extensive stone quarrying and mushrooming of high-rises as part of tourism, and illegal forest land acquisition by private parties are the major reasons for the recent floods in the state."

Gadgil said that the report had very specifically pointed that if the stone quarrying was not stopped, it might eventually lead to natural calamities "like the one happening in the state today". However, the establishments turned a deaf ear to the recommendations. According to Gadgil, a total of 1,650 excavators were deployed for stone quarrying and mining, of which only 150 were given permissions.

The ecologist Madhav Gadgil said that extensive stone quarrying and mushrooming of high-rises as part of tourism, and illegal forest land acquisition by private parties are the major reasons for the recent floods in the state of Kerala.

India's armed services are stepping up efforts to rescue thousands of people stranded by flooding in southern Kerala state that has killed more than 350 people. Some 800,000 people have been displaced and over 350 have died in the worst flooding in a century in southern India's Kerala state, as authorities rushed to bring drinking water to the most affected areas

Expressing grief over the situation in Kerala, Gadgil said, "The government should at least now stop all the illegal stone quarrying activities after having faced the consequences. Although it is late, the government must act on the recommendations ..."

9.3 MADHAV GADGIL PREDICTIONS ON GOA:

Gadgil had done extensive study on Goa's environment based on the data provided by iron ore mining companies in their Environment Impact Assessment (EIA) reports in 2011. He had then said the mining companies submitted false information in their EIA reports. "In Goa, they had asked me to look into the impact of mining on environment. Every EIA suppressed fact about hydrological impact of mining," the Gadgil said. "On sadas (plains) of Goa there are a lot of streams which are originating but they don't mention about them in their EIA reports. All kind of false statements are made in these reports," he said

Ecologist Madhav Gadgil has warned Goa may face the same fate as the flood-battered in Kerala, if it does not take precautions on the environmental front.

Goa, too, is witnessing activities which are driven by greed for unlimited profits, who headed a committee that authored a widely debated study on the Western Ghats a few years ago. Certainly all sorts of problems are beginning to surface on the environmental front in the Western Ghats. Goa, of course, does not have Western Ghats as high in Kerala, but It is sure that Goa will also experience all sorts of problems" Gadgil said, reacting to the worst-ever floods in the southern state. Gadgil said the reason for not taking any environmental precaution (in general) is purely greed for unlimited profits. There is also enormous profit in the business of stone quarrying with very little investment," he added while talking about rampant hill in the WesternGhats. The greed for enormous profits has been allowed to go on unchecked, which has actually worsened economic disparity in the society. "So now those who are making money through these means are even more effective in getting the government allows this kind of rampant illegal behavior".

The ecologist said governments have been lax on implementing environmental norms. "The central government is actually bending over backwards to make sure the National Green Tribunal does not function properly." Now it's the time that the T government should at least now stop all the illegal stone quarrying activities after having faced the consequences in Kerala. Although it is late, the government must act on the recommendations of the ecologist Madhav Gadgil.

9.4 INDIAN HEAT WAVE:

In May 2015, India was struck by a severe heat wave. As of 3 June 2015, it has caused the deaths of at least 2,500 people in multiple regions. The heat wave occurred during the Indian dry season, which typically lasts from March to July with peak temperatures in April and May. Although it typically remains hot until late October, Indian monsoons often provide some respite from the heat.

The South Indian states of Andhra Pradesh and the neighboring Telangana, where more than 1,735 and 585 people died respectively, were the areas most affected by the heat wave. Other casualties were from the eastern states of West Bengal and Odisha. The high demand for electricity to power air conditioning led to power outages in some cities. The 2015 heat wave has had the highest recorded temperatures since 1995.

Starting in April 2023, a record-breaking heat wave has affected many Asian countries, including India, Bangladesh, China, Thailand and Vietnam.

Several regional temperature records have been set. The heat wave has caused multiple deaths due to heat stroke and has prompted health warnings and power outages across multiple countries.

A May 2023 study by the World Weather Attribution found that the heat wave was made at least 30 times more likely by climate change in India and Bangladesh, and that climate change raised temperatures by at least 2 C (3.6°F) in many parts of Asia in April2023.

As of 19 June 2023, 119 people in Uttar Pradesh and 47 people in Bihar had died due to heat-related illnesses. Around 400 people were hospitalised in Uttar Pradesh in the same time period. India is among the countries expected to be worst affected by the impacts of the climate crisis, according to the Intergovernmental Panel on Climate Change. There is every need that the government should take necessary steps to address the heat wave and the surge in deaths.

9.5 KASHMIR FLOODS (2014):

Areas affected: Srinagar, Bandipur, Rajouri etc.

Death toll: 500 plus

The floods caused by continuous torrential rainfall, in the Kashmir region in September 2014 that suffered from massive floods, leading to the death of around 500 people. Hundreds of people were trapped in their homes for days, without food and water. Around 2600 villages were affected in Jammu and Kashmir. In Kashmir itself, 390 villages were completely submerged in water. Many parts of Srinagar were also submerged by the floods. Around 50 bridges were damaged across the state, and the damage of properties was estimated between Rs. 5000 cr and 6000 crore.

Anthropogenic causes of the 2014 floods in Kashmir

- Encroachment on the banks of Jhelum River.
- Rapid, unplanned, and accelerated urbanisation.
- Conversion of Wetlands into Agriculture and Built-up Areas (Loss of Wetlands).
- Degradation of floodplain along the Jhelum River.
- Deforestation.
- Construction of Railway line

9.6 UTTARKHAND FLASH FLOODS (2013):

Areas affected: Gobindghat, Kedar Dome, Rudraprayag district, Uttarakhand, Himachal Pradesh, Western Nepal Death Toll: 5000 plus

In the year 2013, Uttarakhand suffered from a major catastrophic natural disaster in the form of huge and deadly cloudbursts, causing flash floods in River Ganga. Sudden, heavy rains caused dangerous landslides in Uttrakhand, which killed thousands of people and thousands were reported missing. The death toll was estimated to be 5,700. The flash floods and landslides continued for 4 days from 14 to 17 June, 2013. More than 1,00,000 pilgrims were trapped in the valleys that led to the Kedarnath shrine. Today, Uttarakhand Flash Floods are considered the most disastrous floods in the history of India.

On February 7 2021, a glacier broke in the Tapovan-Reni area of Chamoli district which led to massive flooding in Dhauliganga and Alaknanda river. Flash floods and landslides caused by heavy rains in Uttarakhand have claimed the lives of 54 people in the last few days. A total of 19 people have sustained injuries in various incidents while five are still reported missing.

The floods in Uttarakhand can be prevented as detailed below:

- Avoid building in flood prone areas unless you elevate and reinforce your home.
- Elevate the furnace, water heater, and electric panel if susceptible to flooding.
- Install "Check Valves" in sewer traps to prevent floodwater from backing up into the drains of your home.

Flood control infrastructure, such as levees, dams, seawalls, and tide gates, work as physical barriers to prevent rising or running water from causing flooding. Other measures, such as pump stations and channels, help reduce flooding.

9.7 THE INDIAN OCEAN TSUNAMI (2004):

Areas affected: Parts of southern India and Andaman Nicobar Islands, Sri Lanka, Indonesia etc.

Death toll: 2.3 lakh people.

Following a major earthquake in 2004, there was a huge tsunami in the Indian Ocean, causing immense loss of life and property in India and the neighbouring countries – Sri Lanka and Indonesia. On December 26, 2004, a 9.3-magnitude massive undersea earthquake struck off the coast of Sumatra, Indonesia. The earthquake had its epicenter in the ocean bed which led to this destructive tsunami. The magnitude was measured between 9.1 and 9.3 and it lasted for almost 10 minutes. It was the third largest earthquake in the world ever recorded. The impact was equivalent to the energy of 23,000 Hiroshima-type atomic bombs. More than 2 lakh people were killed.

Like the earthquakes that generate most tsunamis, scientists cannot predict when and where the next tsunami will strike. But, the Tsunami Warning Centers know which earthquakes are likely to generate tsunamis and can issue tsunami messages when they think a tsunami is possible.

Historical records show where earthquakes frequently occur. Plate tectonic theory also predicts where earthquakes will occur. Neither historical records nor current scientific theory can accurately tell us when earthquakes will occur. Therefore, tsunami prediction can only be done after an earthquake has occurred.

Being a coastal city, Mumbai is also at risk of tsunamis, with the west coast being more vulnerable because of its high population density, while the east coast, with its mangroves and salt pans, is considered safer.

In the area you have selected (Goa) tsunami hazard is classified as medium according to the information that is currently available. This means that there is more than a 10% chance of a potentially damaging tsunami occurring in the next 50 years.

9.8 GUJARAT EARTHQUAKE (2001):

Areas affected: Bhuj, Ahmedabad, Gandhinagar, Kutch, Surat, Surendranagar district, Rajkot district, Jamnagar and Jodia

Death toll: 20,000 plus

Gujarat was affected by a massive earthquake on the morning of 26 January 2001, the day on which India was celebrating its 51st Republic Day. The earthquake's intensity was in the range of 7.6 to 7.9 on the Richter Scale and lasted for 2 minutes. The impact was so great that almost 20,000 people lost their lives. It was estimated that around 167,000 were injured and nearly 400,000 were left homeless in this natural disaster.

9.9 MAHARASHTRA FLOODS (2005):

The 2005 Maharashtra floods refers to the flooding of many parts of the Indian state of Maharashtra including large areas of the metropolis Mumbai, a city located on the coast of the Arabian Sea, on the Western coast of India, in which approximately 1,094 people died. From the July 26, 2005, killer Mumbai floods to the ongoing situation in Assam, the country has witnessed many water-related catastrophes over the years. A large number of people were stranded on the roads, lost their homes while many walked long distances back home from work that evening. The floods were caused by the eighth heaviest-ever recorded 24-hour rainfall figure of 944 mm (37.17 inches) which lashed the metropolis on 26 July 2005, and intermittently continued for the next day. 644mm (25.35 inches) was received within the 12-hour period between 8 am and 8 pm. Torrential rainfall continued for the next week.

Around 670,000 people got affected by the first wave. The second wave of the floods, which lasted from June 2022 to September 2022, due to "Monsoon season", caused the Brahmaputra, Barak and other major rivers in the state to overflow which eroded the river banks and also the houses present there.

The most flood-affected state in India falls under the Ganga River basins and Brahmaputra. The Indo-Gangetic- Brahmaputra plains in North and Northeast India carry nearly 60% of India's total river flow.

The most affected regions due to the floods in India include Kerala, Assam, West Bengal, Orissa, Andhra Pradesh, Uttar Pradesh, Haryana, Punjab, Bihar, and Gujarat. Gujarat, Telangana and Maharashtra remain the worst affected. By India Today Web Desk: As many as five states are reeling under heavy rain and flood-like situations. In Gujarat, at least 60 people have died and in parts of Telangana, houses have been inundated.

Bihar is India's most flood-prone state. The people of Bihar suffer from recurring floods and more than 76% of the population of North Bihar lives under the recurring threat of flood devastation.

The list of countries ranked by the percentage of the population at risk is topped by the Netherlands, followed by Bangladesh. These countries are the only two in the world that have more than half of their population at risk due to flooding.

9.10 BHOPAL DISASTER (1984):

The Bhopal disaster, also referred to as the Bhopal gas tragedy, was a gas leak incident on the night of 2–3 December 1984 at the Union Carbide India Limited (UCIL) pesticide plant in Bhopal, Madhya Pradesh, India. It was considered as of 2010 to be the world's worst industrial disaster. Over 500,000 people were exposed to methyl isocyanate (MIC) gas. The highly toxic substance made its way into and around the shanty towns located near the plant.

Estimates vary on the death toll. The official immediate death toll was 2,259. The government of Madhya Pradesh confirmed a total of 3,787 deaths related to the gas release. A government affidavit in 2006 stated that the leak caused 558,125 injuries, including 38,478 temporary partial injuries and approximately 3,900 severely and permanently disabling injuries. Others estimate that 8,000 died within two weeks, and another 8,000 or more have since died from gas-related diseases.

The Indian government and local activists argue that slack management and deferred maintenance created a situation where routine pipe maintenance caused a backflow of water into a MIC tank, triggering the disaster. Union Carbide Corporation (UCC) argues water entered the tank through an act of sabotage.

9.11 CHERNOBYL DISASTER (1986):

The Chernobyl disaster, also referred to as the Chernobyl accident, was a catastrophic nuclear accident. It occurred on 25–26 April 1986 in the No. 4 light water graphite moderated reactor at the Chernobyl Nuclear Power Plant near the now-abandoned town of Pripyat, in northern Ukrainian Soviet Socialist Republic, Soviet Union, approximately 104 km (65 mi) north of Kiev. The event occurred during a late-night safety test which simulated astation blackout power-failure, in the course of which safety systems were intentionally turned off. A combination of inherent reactor design flaws and the reactor operators arranging the core in a manner contrary to the checklist for the test, eventually resulted in uncontrolled reaction conditions. Water flashed into steam generating a destructive steam explosion and a subsequent open-air graphite fire.

During the accident, steam-blast effects caused two deaths within the facility; one immediately after the explosion, and the other, compounded by a lethal dose of radiation. Over the coming days and weeks, 134 servicemen were hospitalized with acute radiation sickness (ARS), of which28 firemen and employees died in the days-to-months afterward from the radiation effects. Among the wider population, an excess of 15 childhood thyroid cancer deaths were documented as of 2011.

9.12 MINIMATA DISASTRES (1956):

It is now 50 years since the most horrific mercury poisoning disaster the world has ever seen took place in Minamata, Japan. In May 1956, four patients from the city of Minamata on the west coast of the southern Japanese island of Kyushu were admitted to hospital with the same severe and baffling symptoms.

Minamata is a small factory town. Minamata Bay is a bay on the west coast of Kyūshū island, located in Kumamoto Prefecture, Japan. The poisoning of Minamata Bay had a large impact on Japanese culture as well.

Minamata is a small factory town. Minamata Bay is a bay on the west coast of Kyūshū island, located in Kumamoto Prefecture, Japan Minamata disease. Minamata Bay was heavily polluted in the 1950s and 1960s by wastewater, mixed with mercury dumped into Hyakken Harbour from the Chisso Corporation's factory in Minamata, particularly by methyl mercury.

Methyl mercury poisoning in Japan caused by environmental pollution. Minamata disease (M. d.) is methyl mercury (MeHg) poisoning that occurred in humans who ingested fish and shellfish contaminated by MeHg discharged in waste water from a chemical plant (Chisso Co. Ltd.).

Minamata disease is a disease of the central nervous system, a poisoning caused by long-term consumption, in large amounts, of fish and shellfish from Minamata Bay.

Minamata disease, sometimes referred to as Chisso-Minamata disease, is a neurological syndrome caused by severe mercury poisoning. Symptoms include ataxia, numbness in the hands and feet, general muscle weakness, narrowing of the field of vision and damage to hearing and speech.

9.13 SOME POLLUTION EFFECTS IN CITIES OF INDIA:

Air pollution is a significant environmental health concern for both the developing and the developed world. The World Health Organization (WHO) estimates that

2 million people die prematurely due to air pollution. The WHO ranks air pollution as the 13thleading cause of world-wide mortality, with 527,000 people annually dying prematurely in India due to air pollution.

“Ambient air pollution alone caused some 4.2 million deaths in 2016, while household air pollution from cooking with polluting fuels and technologies caused an estimated 3.8 million deaths in the same period,” said by WHO.

According to the report by World Health Organization (WHO), Delhi and Varanasi are among the 14 Indian cities that figured in a list of 20 most polluted cities in the world in terms of PM2.5 levels in 2016.

Particulate matter is basically a mixture of extremely small particles and liquid droplets like acids, chemicals, gas, water, metals, soil dust particles, etc., the measurement of which gives an idea of the pollution of a city. It is also known as particle pollution or PM.

WHO highlighted that air pollution is mainly responsible for non-communicable diseases (NCDs), causing an estimated one-quarter (24%) of all adult deaths from heart disease, 25% from stroke, 43% from chronic obstructive pulmonary diseases and 29% from lung cancer.

"WHO estimates that around 7 million people die every year from exposure to fine particles in polluted air that penetrate deep into the lungs and cardiovascular system, causing diseases including stroke, heart disease, lung cancer, chronic obstructive pulmonary diseases and respiratory infections, including pneumonia,"

As per the Lancet 2022 study, air pollution is estimated to have caused around 1.7 million premature deaths in India in 2019, accounting for nearly 17.8 per cent of the total deaths recorded in the country that year, the highest in the world. The 2022 report is based on PM2. 5 data from 7,323 cities and 131 countries. Abysmal statistics showed that Bhiwadi in Rajasthan with PM levels of 92.7 was found to be the most polluted city in India and third most polluted city in the world.

The biggest pollution problem in India is Illegal dumping of raw sewage, silt, and garbage into rivers and lakes severely contaminated India's waters. The near-total absence of pipe planning and an inadequate waste management system are only exacerbating the situation. Every day, a staggering 40 million litres of wastewater enter rivers and other water bodies.

Air pollution can also cause long-term damage to people's nerves, brain, kidneys, liver, and other organs. Some scientists suspect air pollutants cause birth defects. Nearly 2.5 million people die worldwide each year from the effects of outdoor or indoor air pollution.

9.13.1 BANGALORE CITY:

In spite of the fact that Bangalore has the unique distinction of gaining many adjectives including 'Air Conditioned City of India' , 'Garden City', etc., It is also gaining another dubious distinction as 'Allergy City'. This city has the highest atmospheric pollution which is responsible for a large proportion of the population suffering from various types of allergies. Because of the numerous parks and gardens-grasses, weeds and trees, atmospheric pollen occurs abundantly. This causes allergic symptoms in sensitive individuals.

Bangalore has one of the highest incidences of asthma in the country and is also referred to as the asthma capital of the country with 25 per cent of cases reported from the city. In 2005, six lakh people were diagnosed with asthma in the city. The primary cause of the condition is pollution, which increases the allergic conditions in the respiratory tract. An increasing number of children are becoming patients of this condition. The causes of asthma in Bangalore is due to low density of air caused by regular rains, the pollens from Green cover that increase allergy, continuous construction of buildings resulting in dust, and pollution.

Sept. 6, 2022, at 2:24 a.m. BENGALURU, India (AP) — Life for many in the southern Indian city of Bengaluru was disrupted on Tuesday after two days of torrential rains set off long traffic snarls, widespread power cuts and heavy floods that swept into homes and submerged roads. Bengaluru, famed as the 'Silicon Valley of India' and the country's leading information technology exporter, had large portions of the city underwater for two days (29 and 30 August 2022). Unprecedented and relentless rains, said to be the third heaviest ever recorded in Bengaluru, inundated the city.

Flood-prone areas with 4 centimeters of rain include: KR Puram, Mahadevapura, Vignan Nagar, ITPB main road, and Tin factory. If the rain goes up to 5-centimetre, areas like, Bellandur, HAL second stage, and Doddanekkundi will be hit.

The Bangalore city is flooded due to the Outer Ring Road (ORR), also known as the Dr. Puneeth Rajkumar Ring Road, which connects the city to its tech parks, frequently floods as a result of a lack of infrastructure. Some believe that people are bothered about the city being flooded only because it affects the productivity of the IT hub in the city. Because there are no culverts along this stretch, rainwater and sewage water are forced to build up, which results in waterlogging. The highway acts as a dam for the water. According to reports, Bengaluru's drainage infrastructure is unprepared to handle periods of unexpectedly severe rainfall. Garbage frequently clogs drains, which limits the flow of sewage, and they are too small to support the weight of the expanding population.

Solution: Flooding can be avoided if each plot is given responsibility for the stormwater by storing or recharging into a well every drop of rain that falls on the land, according to Citizen Matters. Additionally, it is recommended that permeable surfaces rather than full concrete be utilised in locations such as parking lots, footpaths, walking and jogging lanes, common areas in apartments, companies, and other large structures.

9.13.2 KANPUR CITY:

The city of Kanpur in the north Indian state Uttar Pradesh is famed for its leather industry, meeting national and international demands for superior quality leather.

It is a source of hazardous pollution that, environmentalists say, is gradully killing the city.Each day, the tanneries pump out about 30 crore liters of polluted water into the adjacent Ganges river. The city's water treatment unit, however, has a capacity of treating 17 crore litres per day. Kanpur also generates 400 tons of solid waste. The rampant pollution has contaminated ground water sources.

There are reports of increasing deformities among newborn babies. Farmers complain their fields are turning toxic.

The city of Kanpur in northern India has an annual PM2.5 level of 173 micrograms per cubic meter, far higher than the WHO's recommendation of no more than 10 mcg per cubic meter. The PM2.5 includes pollutants like sulfate, nitrate and black carbon, which pose the greatest risk to human health.

9.13.3 FARIDABAD CITY:

The National Capital Region (NCR) cities of Gurgaon and Faridabad were among the most polluted cities in the country, shows a report on air pollution data compiled by Greenpeace India.The report vindicates what the city residents have been crying about for years—that pollution level has reached dangerous levels and serious measures will have to be taken by the government to bring the situation under control.

The report revealed that the average level of PM10 in Faridabad was 272 making it the second most-polluted city in the country. **Particulate matter less than 10 microns in diameter, about 1/7th the thickness of the human hair, are known as PM10.** It is among the most harmful of all air pollutants. When inhaled these particles evade the respiratory system's natural defenses and lodge deep in the lungs. PM10 is often responsible for much of the haze that we call smog.

9.13.4 DELHI CITY:

Delhi, the national capital of the country, is being tagged as one of the most heavily polluted capital cities in the world. It is the world's worst city in terms of air pollution, with an unhealthy air quality index for most of the year. Thus, today, one of the biggest threats to the welfare of the people of Delhi and the city as a whole is pollution of various types.

- According to the Ambient Air Pollution (AAP) report for the year 2014, Delhi had PM 2.5 pollution levels, which is the highest in the world. The highest concentration of PM 2.5 form of air pollution is supposed to be a very serious matter and can lead to respiratory diseases and other health problems like lung cancer.
- Carbon monoxide (CO), a dangerous gas emission, is around 6,000 microgram per cubic metre in Delhi, which is much above the the safe level of 2,000 microgram per cubic metre.
- The level of nitrogen dioxide (NO2) has also been increasing.
- According to the Ministry of Earth Sciences, Delhi's air quality index (AQI) is 121, which is described as "poor." The AQI is an index for reporting daily air quality, about how clean or polluted the air is.
- Earthquake in Delhi: Delhi is indeed prone to earthquakes. It falls in seismic zone 4 along the Aravali fault line, where the probability of temblors of severe intensity is high. Delhi lies among the high-risk zones. "Delhi is located in zone IV which has fairly high seismicity where the general occurrence of earthquakes is of 5-6 magnitude, a few of magnitude 6-7 and occasionally of 7-8 magnitude," the city government's District Disaster Management Authority (DDMA) said. Well, if the buildings in the city are earthquake-resistant, the situation wouldn't probably turn catastrophic, as it happened in Turkey and Syria.

Months after Turkey was badly devastated by Earthquake, India has recently felt a scary tremor late at night on March 22, 2023. The Earthquake with Rector scale 7.7 has ignited fear in the minds of people who suddenly remembered the prediction made by a Frank Hogarbeits the Dutch researcher during the time of the Turkey earthquake. Here is everything you need to know about the prediction for India and Pakistan.

About 10:30 p.m. on Tuesday, strong earthquake tremors were detected in the national capital of Delhi and the NCR(National Capital Region). In addition to this, tremors from an earthquake were also felt in numerous North Indian states. Long periods of chaos were experienced in different parts of the country. People were spotted coming out from their residences and workplaces. Islamabad, the capital of neighboring Pakistan, also experienced tremors. The prediction of Dutch researcher Frank Hogerbeets is being addressed in such a circumstance.

9.13.5 AGRA CITY:

Taj Mahal is situated in Agra. The air in this place contains serious levels of sulphur and nitrogen oxides. This is due to the large number of power plants and industries set up around this area. All these led to acid rain. Acid rain reacted with the marble (calcium carbonate) of Taj Mahal. This caused damage to this wonderful structure, which had attracted many people from different parts of the world.

One of the seven Wonders of the World, the Taj Mahal flanks a garbage-strewn river and is often enveloped by dust and smog from belching smokestacks and vehicles in the northern city of Agra. The change in color has not come out of the blue. Environmentalists and historians have long warned about the risk of soot and fumes from factories and tanneries dulling the ivory monument.

9.13.6 HOLY RIVER YAMUNA SUFFERING FROM FOAM:

The Yamuna also known as the Jamuna is the longest and the second largest tributary river of the Ganges (Ganga) in northern India. Originating from the Yamunotri Glacier at a height of 6,387 metres on the southwestern slopes of Banderpooch peaks in the uppermost region of the Lower Himalaya in Uttarakhand, Yamunotri temple, a shrine dedicated to the goddess, Yamuna is one of the holiest shrines in Hinduism

The river Yamuna enters Delhi from Palla village. 22 drains fall into the Yamuna. Out of these, 18 drains fall directly into river and 4 through Agra and Gurgaon canal. Lack of sufficient number of sewage treatment plants has led to the increase in the polluted stretch of the Yamuna.

According to the Centre for Science and Environment, approximately 75 to 80 percent of the river's pollution is the result of raw sewage, industrial runoff and the garbage thrown into the river and it totals over 3 billion liters of waste per day.

Pink foam from toxic industrial waste floating in the river Yamuna at Wazirabad in North Delhi is yet another reminder of how polluted the river is.

Nearly One billion Hindus worship the Yamuna River as a goddess. They consider it nearly as sacred as the mighty Ganges, and yet it is dying. The stretch that meanders through New Delhi teems with filth and toxins, and its surface bubbles with thick, white foam.

9.13.7 AMARAVATHI – THE STATE CAPITAL OF ANDHRA PRADESH

India's newest state capital Amaravati is being planned on the banks of the river Krishna in the southern state of Andhra Pradesh, on land that floods thrice in an average year, and is dry and often drought-prone the rest of the time.

Amaravati is located between the Krishna River and some low hills of the Deccan Plateau. If it rains in the hills, then the amount of water that will reach the city, and then open the gates to a diversion canal, check the reservoir capacity and pump if necessary. Similarly, the smart system can manage the sewerage system, so that more pumps work when there is a lot of water flowing.

Why is Amaravati being built on such a vulnerable spot? The only defence of the policymakers is that it is the best spot available, even when they know their new capital may run short of water despite being on the banks of the Krishna.

Amaravati is located at a point where Kondaveeti Vagu, a small river, joins the Krishna. "Together with its own tributaries, Kondaveeti Vagu flows across the capital city and causes inundation over about 13,500 acres of land every year during the monsoon season. The inundation of the low-lying areas within the capital city development area will usually last for 5 to 7 days during each spell of heavy rain and this occurs two to three times annually."

And when it rains heavily and upper riparian states let the water out of their dams, the new city may be flooded. That happens now to the farms over which Amaravati is being planned. One of the flood management strategies listed in the Master Plan is to fix a minimum platform height of 25 metres above sea level for future developments in the city. "As a rule of thumb, the existing ground level should be topped up to a higher level than the maximum predicted flood level in each zone," the plan states.

In addition to raising the city, other strategies include reinforcing and realigning the existing Krishna river bund; detain storm water in ponds within the capital and the catchment area; conserve raw water using reservoirs; provide a green belt along the water bodies; and discharge excess water into the Krishna.

In all, 30,300 families residing on the banks of the Godavari, island villages, and in the low-lying areas in West Godavari and Eluru districts, have been affected due to unprecedented floods. Floods and cyclones are major natural disasters in Andhra Pradesh State and have a great impact on loss of property, infrastructure and agriculture. Identification of the flood-prone areas and the risk associated would offer significant help for the planners to devise area-specific mitigation measures. The 1977 Andhra Pradesh cyclone was a devastating tropical cyclone that hit Andhra Pradesh in November 1977, killing at least 10,000 people. The worst affected areas were in the Krishna River delta region. Budameru is a rivulet in Krishna district which originates in the hills surrounding Mylavaram and empties itself into Kolleru Lake. Budameru is also known as "The Sorrow of Vijayawada".

Andhra Pradesh has a coastline of 974 km, and it is highly prone to cyclones of various degrees. Floods and cyclones are major natural disasters in Andhra Pradesh State and have a great impact on loss of property, infrastructure and agriculture.

Visakhapatnam city, its suburbs, Prakasam and Guntur districts and the upland areas of West Godavari district and Adilabad district in Telangana are likely to face water problem, according to a study conducted by a former Director of the India Meteorological Department P.V. Rama Rao.

Andhra Pradesh falls in zone – II and III and is prone to moderate to low risk. The Major earthquake prone areas of Andhra Pradesh are: 1. Ongole This area has faced 12 earthquakes in the last 30 years including two big ones in 1967 and 1959 on Richter scale of 5.4 and 5. On January 26, 2020, an earthquake of magnitude 4.7 occurred near Pulichintala project.

Seismic experts say the Amaravati region, the planned capital city of Andhra Pradesh, lies in the earthquake Zone-3, a dangerous zone as per the scientific studies.

In seismic zone III, an earthquake of maximum intensity 7 on the Richter scale can be expected. A major part of the country falls in the zone, including Andhra Pradesh.

According to the Hyderabad IIIT Earthquake Engineering Research Centre head Pradeep Kumar, new buildings should be constructed according to earthquake resistant standards and its guidelines.

Interestingly, the Sivarama Krishnan committee constituted by the Union Government of India to suggest the place to build the capital city of Andhra Pradesh and submitted its report on 27 August 2014 to the Home Minister Rajnath Singh in New Delhi. The Sivarama Krishnancommittee objected Vijayawada to be the capital, in the context of the AP government transferring certain departments to Vijayawada, declaring it as the future capital. **The Committee said that the capital between Vijayawada-Guntur is incorrect** because it would bring up economic and environmental problems. It also opined that farmers and laborers are more in Krishna and Guntur districts and would make it difficult for land acquisition and would benefit only realtors and the traffic in Vijayawada-Guntur-Mangalagiri- Tenali cities is likely to be higher.

Sivarama Kishnan committee opined that the capital could be between Marturu and Vinukonda. It also proposed Musunuru, Mangalagiri, Macherla, Gollapally, Vinukonda, Marturu, Donakonda, Pulichintala as suitable for Capital regions. But the Government of Andhra Pradesh neglected the committees report.

RED SANDAL WOOD IN ANDHRA PRADESH:

Pterocarpus santalinus, with the common names **red sanders, red saunders, Yerra Chandanam, Chenchandanam, red sandalwood, Rakta Chandana, and saunderswood**, is a species of Pterocarpus endemic to the southern Eastern Ghats mountain range of South India. Red Sandal wood is a native and endemic to India and can only be found in the southern parts of the Eastern Ghats. It is a small tree that grows to 5-8 meters in height and has a dark grayish bark.

"Red Sandalwood is native and endemic to India and can only be found in the Seshachalam hills andNallamala forest region of the southern Indian state of Andhra Pradesh". It was listed as an endangered species by the IUCN (International Union for Conservation of Nature) because of overexploitation for its timber in South India. Red sanders is endemic in Seshachalam, Veliganda, Lankamala, and Palakonda hill ranges in districts of Kadapa, Chittoor, and Kurnool in Rayalaseema region and parts of Nellore and Prakasam Districts of Andhra Pradesh and Javajimalai in Tamil Nadu.

Basically, they are only grown in Eastern Ghats as the soil in the area — its water content, acidity, aeration and the availability of nutrients only. Recommended for plantation on lateritic loam, quartzite shale and lime stone.

It requires perfect drainage and is found mainly on stony or gravelly soils. It is fast-growing when young, reaching 5 metres (16 ft) tall in three years, even on degraded soils. It is not frost tolerant, being killed by temperatures of "1°C.

Facing resource crunch, Andhra Pradesh government will aggressively promote red-sanders plantation in a big way even as it will install CCTVs to keep a round-the-clock vigil at depots storing this precious wood.[PTI Last Updated: Aug 08, 2014, 06:09 PM IST]. Red Sandal wood being the costliest raw material, the bulk plantation shall provides a platform for better management of the market dynamics relating to demand, supply and cost.

Grow Red Sanders to become Billionaires: AP Forest Forces Chief Rizvi

MN Samdani | TNN | Jul 15, 2018, 14:30 IST

I) GUNTUR: In what could be an interesting appeal, **state forest forces chief Md Ilyas Rizvi** has called upon the people to grow precious plants like red sanders, sandal wood and teak in the barren and waste lands to reap rich in the future. Scotching the apprehensions about growing red sanders in private land, Rizvi said that absolutely there is no ban on cultivation of any kind of wood.

In an exclusive interview with TOI,(Times of India) **Principal Chief Conservator of Forests (PCCF) Rizvi** said that forest department is ready to supply any plant if people came forward to grow them in their backyard. "People are required to take permission to sell the red-sander or sandal wood grown in private land which we will give if they produce proper documents of cultivation. It is not a big issue," he promised.

He said that there is no need for anyone to seek permission for growing the plants including red sanders.

Rizvi said that people would always prefer gifting gold and land to their children and grandchildren thinking that such things would help their kin in need in future and make them economically stable. "What they actually do not know is that their investment in such things did not make their kid really rich because of the inflation. **A gift of one acre of red sander will make their kid a true billionaire," said Rizvi.**

He said that middle class people who purchase house-plots too should think of growing some plants in the vacant land till they go for construction of house as it helps those making little monies without much investment. "Massive extent of land in real-estate ventures in the state has been kept barren. It is really bad practice," said Rizvi.

II) Speaking to The Hindu , Chief Conservator of Forests (Tirupati Wildlife Circle), Mr. P.V. Chalapathi Rao said there were so many fallacies among the public about the commercial exploitation of red sanders plantations.

"They have formulated wrong opinions over the years that growing red sanders is a crime, or its trade is prohibited and involves criminal action by police and forest departments. Farmers and private planters should realize that just by paying a user charge of Rs.10 or 20, they can grow red sanders and sell them at any price of their choice to anyone anywhere. It will be like growing any other agriculture crop," he said.

The official said there was no need for planters to inform the Forest Department before going in for red sanders plantation. "Whenever they want to cut the trees and sell them, all they have to do is to get transit permits from the Forest Department. This is for the safety of their own material during transportation" Mr Rao added.

9.14 CONCLUSIONS:

Over population and pollution are potent ecological forces impinging upon man by affecting the quality of the environment. All efforts aimed at bringing more and more people above the poverty line actually increase the pressure on natural resources.

As pollution is one of the biggest problems the world is facing today, it is also affecting our daily lives economically and physically. A polluted environment also leads to diseases that are around us. Yet most people have no awareness of this grave issue at hand. Many activities can be carried out by both the common citizen and countries to help improve the world's environmental pollution. Some initiatives should be taken to fight this cause.

- First, an individual can play his role by proving him to be a good citizen. We should not exceed the limits defined by the law regarding noise, air and water pollution.
- The widespread use of polythene bags should be stopped as they are one of the main causes of pollution; the option of cloth bags is safer.
- Garbage should be recycled instead of throwing it away. Dry garbage can be used in construction of roads and wet garbage can be used as urea in our lawns.
- Vehicles should be kept in good condition so that they do not become a cause of air pollution. The government should take steps to prevent pollution.
- Noise pollution can also be reduced considerably by passing stringent laws of not exceeding the limit. Sewage disposal treatment should have specific laws for even a good sewerage system can also help prevent a number of diseases and germs.
- Over Exploitation: The IPBES(Intergovernmental Platform for Biodiversity and Ecosystem Services) suggests that fishing has had a larger impact on marine ecosystems than any other human activity: 33 percent of marine fish stocks are currently overfished, and 60 percent are being fished to their sustainable limits. Poaching and hunting, too, are driving many mammals to the brink of extinction.
- Invasive species: An invasive alien species is a species that has been introduced to a new location and starts to disrupt its new habitat. These species can threaten native biodiversity by out-competing them for resources, and they're spreading ever more quickly as international travel and trade expands. A recent study found that one-sixth of the Earth's land surface is highly vulnerable to invasion, including many biodiversity hotspots.
- At the individual level, that could include reducing air travel, buying organic, eating less red meat, avoiding fast fashion, and turning your backyard into a carbon sink.
- At the international and policy level, we need commitments to restore the Earth's ecosystems, following the examples set by the Everglades and farmers in the African Sahel.
- **To conclude, the five biggest Environmental Issues in India today 2023 needs to be addressed stringently by the Government mechanism and policy makers as well.**
    1. Air Pollution
    2. Water Pollution,

3. Food and water shortages,
4. Waste Management,
5. Biodiversity loss: Land use change, pollution, poor water quality, chemical and waste contamination, climate change and other causes of ecosystem degradation all contribute to biodiversity loss and, can pose considerable threats to human health.

If we want to live a healthy and prosperous life, we should first keep our environment and country clean as well as clean world.

******

INDEX

A

Accrued :	Sum of money received or accumulated in regular or increasing amounts over time.
Abode :	A place of residence; a house or home.
Abuse :	Use (something) to bad effect or for a bad purpose; misuse; treat with cruelty or violence.
Admiration:	Pleased Contemplation, Respect & warm approval.
Advocacy :	Public support for or recommendation of a particular cause or policy
Aerosols :	A substance enclosed under pressure and able to be released as a fine spray, typically by means of a propellant gas
Aesthetic :	A set of principles underlying and guiding the work of a particular artist or artistic movement
Aggrandizement :	The action or process of promoting oneself as being powerful or important.
Agrarian :	A person who advocates a redistribution of landed property, especially as part of a social movement.
Aquatic :	An aquatic plant or animal, especially one suitable for a pond or aquarium.
Amoebiasis :	Infection with amoebas, especially as causing dysentery.
Attic :	The dialect of Greek used by the ancient Athenians, the chief literary form of classical Greek; a space in a house just under the roof, often used for storing things.
Ascariasis :	Infection of the intestine with ascarids (parasitic roundworm Ascaris lumbricoides).
Akhirah :	Ākhirah is an Islamic term referring to the afterlife.
Almighty :	Having complete power; Omnipotent; a name or title for God.
Alzheimer's :	Progressive mental deterioration that can occur in middle or old age, due to generalized degeneration of the brain. It is the most common cause of premature senility.
Alleged :	Said, without proof, to have taken place or to have a specified illegal or undesirable quality.
Ambient :	Relating to the immediate surroundings of something.
Ameliorate :	To make a bad or unpleasant situation better.

Animism :	The attribution of a soul to plants, inanimate objects, and natural phenomena; the belief in a supernatural power that organizes and animates the material universe.
Aspires :	Direct one's hopes or ambitions toward achieving something.
Asunder :	Apart.
Assimilate :	Take in and understand fully (information or ideas); (of the body or any biological system) absorb and digest (food or nutrients).
Attainment :	The action or fact of achieving a goal towards which one has worked
Avarice :	Extreme greed for wealth or material gain.

B

Benefactor :	a person who gives money or other help to a person or cause.
Biblical :	Relating to or contained in the Bible.
Bioavailability :	The proportion of a drug or other substance which enters the circulation when introduced into the body and so is able to have an active effect.
Bioconversion :	The conversion of organic matter, such as animal or plant waste, into a source of energy through the action of microorganisms.
Biodiversity :	The variety of life in the world or in a particular habitat or ecosystem
Biotic :	Relating to or resulting from living things, especially in their ecological relations.
Biological :	Relating to biology or living organisms; a therapeutic substance, such as a vaccine or drug, derived from biological sources.
Bioremediation :	The use of either naturally occurring or deliberately introduced microorganisms to consume and break down environmental pollutants, in order to clean a polluted site.
Bounties :	A sum paid for killing or capturing a person or animal; a sum paid to encourage trade.

C

Carcinogens :	A substance capable of causing cancer in living tissue.
Caesar :	A title of Roman emperors, especially those from Augustus to Hadrian
Caliph :	The chief Muslim civil and religious ruler, regarded as the successor Muhammad. The caliph ruled in Baghdad until 1258 and then in Egypt until the Ottoman conquest of 1517; the title was then held by the Ottoman sultans until it was abolished in 1924 by Atatürk.
Cataclysm :	A large-scale and violent event in the natural world.

Catechism :	A summary of the principles of Christian religion in the form of questions and answers, used for religious instruction.
Caulking :	A waterproof filler and sealant, used in building work and repairs; seal (a gap or seam) with a waterproof filler and sealant.
Chaos :	Complete disorder and confusion.
Cereal :	A grain used for food, such as wheat, oats, or corn.
Chlorophyll :	A green pigment, present in all green plants and in cyanobacteria, responsible for the absorption of light to provide energy for photosynthesis. Its molecule contains a magnesium atom held in a porphyrin ring.
Chlorofluorocarbons :	Any of several volatile, inert, saturated compounds of carbon, fluorine, chlorine & hydrogen.
Coliform :	Belonging to a group of rod-shaped bacteria typified by E. coli.
Compassion :	Sympathetic pity and concern for the sufferings or misfortunes of others.
Competitors :	Any person or entity which is a rival against another.
Complimentary :	Expressing a compliment; praising or approving.
Conscious :	Aware of and responding to one's surroundings; awake.
Consciousness :	The state of being awake and aware of one's surroundings.
Consolation :	The comfort received by a person after a loss or disappointment.
Consumerism :	The protection or promotion of the interests of consumers; the preoccupation of society with the acquisition of consumer goods.
Consumption :	The action of using up a resource.
Contaminated :	Having been made impure by exposure to or addition of a poisonous or polluting substance.
Copious :	Abundant in supply or quantity.
Cardinal :	Of the greatest importance; fundamental.
Conversing :	Engage in conversation.
Cosmology :	The science of the origin and development of the universe. Modern astronomy is dominated by the Big Bang theory, which brings together observational astronomy and particle physics.
Cosmic :	Relating to the universe or cosmos, especially as distinct from the earth
Cosmos :	The universe seen as a well-ordered whole; a system of thought.
Covenant :	An agreement; agree by lease, deed, or other legal contract.
Creed :	A system of religious belief; a faith.
Creatures :	An animal, as distinct from a human being.
Culminated :	Reach a climax or point of highest development

D

Decay :	Rot or decompose through the action of bacteria and fungi; the state or process of rotting or decomposition.
Deceit :	The action or practice of deceiving someone by concealing or misrepresenting the truth.
Degradation :	The condition or process of degrading or being degraded.
Deeds :	A legal document that is signed and delivered, especially one regarding the ownership of property or legal rights.
Defilements :	The action of defiling or the state of being defiled.
Depletion :	Reduction in the number or quantity of something.
Despoiler :	To ruin, especially by destroying or removing what is valuable: "a landscape that had been raped and despoiled by coal mining" (George Black).
Desertification :	The process by which fertile land becomes desert, typically as a result of drought, deforestation, or inappropriate agriculture.
Desist :	Stop doing something; cease or abstain
Destroying :	Put an end to the existence of (something) by damaging or attacking it
Deteriorating :	Becoming progressively worse.
Deity :	A God or Goddess (in a polytheistic religion).
Dhammapada :	Is a collection of sayings of the Buddha in verse form and one of the most widely read and best known Buddhist scriptures. The original version of the **Dhammapada** is in the KhuddakaNikaya, a division of the Pali Canon of Theravada Buddhism.
Disruption :	Disturbance or problems which interrupt an event, activity, or process
Divine :	Like God or a God; Excellent; Delightful.
Diligent :	Having or showing care and conscientiousness in one's work or duties.
Dissolution :	the closing down or dismissal of an assembly, partnership.
Doctrines :	A belief or set of beliefs held and taught by a Church, political party, or other group.
Domain :	An area of territory owned or controlled by a particular ruler or government.
Doomsday :	The last day of the world's existence; a time or event of crisis or great danger.
Dormant :	Having normal physical functions suspended or slowed down for a period of time; in or as if in a deep sleep.
Dominion :	Sovereignty or control; the territory of a sovereign or government.

DNA : Deoxyribonucleic acid, a self-replicating material which is present in nearly all living organisms as the main constituent of chromosomes. It is the carrier of genetic informationThe fundamental and distinctive characteristics or qualities of someone or something, especially when regarded as unchangeable.

Dualistic : 1. A theory that considers reality to consist of two irreducible elements or modes. 2. The quality or state of being dual or of having a dual nature. 3. A doctrine that the universe is under the dominion of two opposing principles one of which is good and the other evil.

Dynamics : The branch of mechanics concerned with the motion of bodies under the action of forces; the forces or properties which stimulate growth, development, or change within a system or process.

E

Ecology : The branch of biology that deals with the relations of organisms to one another and to their physical surroundings; the political movement concerned with protection of the environment.

Ecosystem : A biological community of interacting organisms and their physical environment; (in general use) a complex network or interconnected system.

Ecumenical : Representing a number of different Christian Churches; promoting or relating to unity among the world's Christian Churches.

Effluents :Liquid waste or sewage discharged into a river or the sea.

Endangered : (of a species) seriously at risk of extinction.

Endeavour : Try hard to do or achieve something; an attempt to achieve a goal.

Entails : Involve (something) as a necessary or inevitable part or consequence; a limitation of the inheritance of property to certain heirs over a number of generations.

Emergence : The process of becoming visible after being concealed; the process of coming into existence or prominence.

Emission : The production and discharge of something, especially gas or radiation; an ejaculation of semen.

Endocrine : Relating to or denoting glands which secrete hormones or other products directly into the blood.

Environment : The surroundings or conditions in which a person, animal, or plant lives or operates; the natural world, as a whole or in a particular geographical area, especially as affected by human activity.

Evolutionary : Relating to or denoting the process by which different kinds of living organism are believed to have developed from earlier forms during the history of the earth; relating to the gradual development of something.

Encephalitis : Inflammation of the brain, caused by infection or an allergic.

Engendered : Cause or give rise to (a feeling, situation, or condition)

Enlightenment : The action of enlightening or the state of being enlightened.

Equanimity : Calmness and composure, especially in a difficult situation.

Enzymatic : Relating to, or Produced by an enzyme.

Enzymes : A substance produced by a living organism which acts as a catalyst to bring about a specific biochemical reaction.

Etiquette : The customary code of polite behaviour in society or among members of a particular profession or group.

Ethics : Moral principles that govern a person's behaviour or the conducting of an activity; the branch of knowledge that deals with moral principles.

Evolution : The process by which different kinds of living organism are believed to have developed from earlier forms during the history of the earth.

Exhibited : Publicly display (a work of art or item of interest) in an art gallery or museum or at a trade fair.

Exhorted : Strongly encourage or urge (someone) to do something.

Exploitation : The action or fact of treating someone unfairly in order to benefit from their work.

Extinct : Having no living members; not having erupted in recorded history.

Extinction : The state or process of being or becoming extinct; reduction to zero in the intensity of light or other radiation as it passes through a medium, due to absorption, reflection, or scattering.

Evangelists : A person who seeks to convert others to the Christian faith, especially by public preaching.

Eventually : In the end, especially after a long delay, dispute, or series of problems

Evolution : The process by which different kinds of living organism are believed to have developed from earlier forms during the history of the earth.

F

Famine : Extreme scarcity of food.

Fodder : Food, especially dried hay or straw, for Cattle and other livestock.

Food chain : The series of processes by which food is grown or produced, sold, and eventually consumed

Food web : A system of interlocking and interdependent food chains.

Forbidden : Not allowed; Banned.

Fosters : Encourage the development of (something, especially something desirable).

Fragmented : Break or cause to break into fragments; *Existing or functioning as though broken into several parts; disorganised; disunified.*

G

Galaxies : A system of millions or billions of stars, together with gas and dust, held together by gravitational attraction.

Genetic mutations : A gene mutation is a permanent alteration in the DNA sequence that makes up a gene, such that the sequence differs from what is found in most people. Mutations range in size; they can affect anywhere from a single DNA building block (base pair) to a large segment of a chromosome that includes multiple genes.

Genesis : The origin or mode of formation of something.

Generosity : The quality of being kind and generous; the quality or fact of being plentiful or large.

Global warming : A gradual increase in the overall temperature of the earth's atmosphere generally attributed to the greenhouse effect caused by increased levels of carbon dioxide, CFCs, and other pollutants.

Giardiasis : Infection of the intestine with a flagellate protozoan, which causes Diarrhoea and other symptoms.

Gratification : Pleasure, especially when gained from the satisfaction of a desire

Greed : Intense and selfish desire for something, especially wealth, power, or food.

H

Habitat : The natural home or environment of an animal, plant, or organism.

Harmony : The combination of simultaneously sounded musical notes to produce a pleasing effect.

Harnessing : Control and make use of (natural resources), especially to produce energy.

Hazardous : Risky; Dangerous.

Herbicides : A substance that is toxic to plants, used to destroy unwanted vegetation

Heritage : Property that is or may be inherited; an inheritance / a special or individual possession; an allotted portion.

Hilarity : Extreme amusement, especially when expressed by laughter.

Homespun : Simple and Unsophisticated.

Hymn : A religious song or poem of praise to God or a God.

I

Ideology : A system of ideas and ideals, especially one which forms the basis of economic or political theory and policy.

Ignite : Catch fire or cause to catch fire.

Illusion : An instance of a wrong or misinterpreted perception of a sensory experience.

Imbibing : Absorb or Assimilate (ideas or knowledge) / (especially of seeds) absorb (water) into ultramicroscopic spaces or pores.

Immanent : Existing or operating within; inherent / (of God) permanently pervading and sustaining the universe.

Inflated : Distended through being filled with air or gas / excessively or unreasonably high.

Inflicting : Cause (something unpleasant or painful) to be suffered by someone or something / impose something unwelcome on.

Insomnia : Habitual sleeplessness; Inability to sleep.

Irradiated : Expose (someone or something) to radiation / illuminate (something) by or as if by shining light on it.

Imploding : Collapse or Cause to collapse violently inwards.

Imminent : About to happen / Overhanging.

Immune : Resistant to a particular infection or toxin owing to the presence of specific antibodies or sensitized white blood cells / protected or exempt, especially from an obligation or the effects of something.

Immutable : Unchanging over time or unable to be changed.

Inalienable : Not subject to being taken away from or given away by the Possessor.

Incidence : The occurrence, rate, or frequency of a disease, crime, or other undesirable thing / the intersection of a line, or something moving in a straight line, such as a beam of light, with a surface.

Indiscriminate : Done at random or without careful judgement / (of a person) not using or exercising discrimination.

Inherited : Receive (money, property, or a title) as an heir at the death of the previous holder / derive (a quality, characteristic, or predisposition) genetically from one's parents or ancestors.

Inorganic : Not consisting of or deriving from living matter / relating to or denoting compounds which are not organic (broadly, compounds not containing carbon).

Innocuous : Not harmful or offensive.

Innately : As an inborn characteristic; naturally.

Insecticides : A substance used for killing insects.

Intensification : The action of making or becoming more intense.

Isotopes : Each of two or more forms of the same element that contain equal numbers of protons but different numbers of neutrons in their nuclei, and hence differ in relative atomic mass but not in chemical properties; in particular, a radioactive form of an element.

Incineration : The destruction of something, especially waste material, by burning.

J

Jataka : Any of the various stories of the former lives of the Buddha found in Buddhist literature

Jurists : An expert in or writer on law / a lawyer or a judge

L

Lymphoma : Cancer of the lymph nodes

Leukaemia : A malignant progressive disease in which the bone marrow and other blood-forming organs produce increased numbers of immature or abnormal leucocytes. These suppress the production of normal blood cells, leading to anaemia and other symptoms.

Lumbering : Moving in a slow, heavy, Awkward way

M

Mammals : A warm-blooded vertebrate animal of a class that is distinguished by the possession of hair or fur, females that secrete milk for the nourishment of the young, and (typically) the birth of live young

Manifestations : An event, action, or object that clearly shows or embodies something abstract or theoretical / the action or fact of showing something / a symptom of an ailment.

Meditative : Relating to or absorbed in meditation or considered thought.

Meditation : The action or practice of meditating / a written or spoken discourse expressing considered thoughts on a subject.

Membranes : A pliable sheet-like structure acting as a boundary, lining, or partition in an organism / a thin pliable sheet of material forming a barrier or lining.

Metabolism : The chemical processes that occur within a living organism in order to maintain life.

Metaphysical : Metaphysics is the branch of philosophy that studies the essence of a thing. This includes questions of being, becoming, existence, and reality.

Mitigating : Make (something bad) less severe, serious, or painful / lessen the gravity of (an offence or mistake).

Miniscule : Extremely small; tiny.

Morality : A particular system of values and principles of conduct.

Manifestation : The action or fact of showing something.

Mythology : A collection of myths, especially one belonging to a particular religious or cultural tradition.

N

Nausea : A feeling of sickness with an inclination to vomit.

Nectars :	The drink that the Greek and Roman gods drank. : a thick juice made from a particular fruit. : a sweet liquid produced by plants and used by bees in making honey.
Nourishment :	The food necessary for growth, health, and good condition / the action of nourishing someone or something.
Nurture :	Care for and protect (someone or something) while they are. Growing

O

Oneness :	The fact or state of being unified or whole, though comprised of two or more parts.
Omnipresent :	Widely or constantly encountered; widespread / (of God) present everywhere at the same time.
Ordains :	Make (someone) a priest or minister; Confer holy orders on / order (something) officially.
Organic :	Relating to or derived from living matter / (of food or farming methods) produced or involving production without the use of chemical fertilizers, pesticides, or other artificial chemicals.
Ozone :	A colourless unstable toxic gas with a pungent odour and powerful oxidizing properties, formed from oxygen by electrical discharges or ultraviolet light. It differs from normal oxygen (O_2) in having three atoms in its molecule (O_3).

P

Pacifist :	A person who believes that war and violence are unjustifiable.
Paradoxical :	Seemingly absurd or self-contradictory.
Partake :	Eat or Drink (something) / join in (an activity).
Pantheism :	A doctrine which identifies God with the universe, or regards the universe as a manifestation of God / the worship or tolerance of many Gods.
Parjanya :	Parjanya (Sanskrit: parjánya) is according to Veda, a deity of rain, the one who fertilizes the earth.
Parasites :	An organism which lives in or on another organism (its host) and benefits by deriving nutrients at the other's expense.
Pastures :	Land covered with grass and other low plants suitable for grazing animals, especially cattle or sheep / used to refer to a person's situation in life.
Patriarch :	The male head of a family or tribe / any of those biblical figures regarded as fathers of the human race, especially Abraham, Isaac, and Jacob, and their forefathers, or the sons of Jacob.

Pedestal : The base or support on which a statue, obelisk, or column is mounted / a position in which someone is greatly or uncritically admired

Perceived : Become aware or conscious of (something); come to realize or understand / interpret or regard (someone or something) in a particular way.

Perched : (of a person) Sit on something high or narrow / (of a building) be situated above or on the edge of something.

Precepts : A general rule intended to regulate behaviour or thought.

Pesticides : A substance used for destroying insects or other organisms harmful to cultivated plants or to animals.

Pervading : Be present and apparent throughout.

Perishable : (especially of food) Likely to decay or go bad quickly.

Petavatthu : The Petavatthu (lit."Ghost Stories") is a Theravada Buddhist scripture, included in the Minor Collection (KhuddakaNikaya) of the Pali Canon's SuttaPitaka. It ostensibly reports stories about and conversations among the Buddha and his disciples, but in fact dates to about 300 BC at the earliest. It is composed of 51 verse narratives describing specifically how the effects of bad acts can lead to rebirth into the unhappy world of petas (ghosts) in the doctrine of karma. More importantly, it details how meritorious actions by the living can benefit such suffering souls.

Plurality : The fact or state of being plural.

Primitive : Relating to, denoting, or preserving the character of an early stage in the evolutionary or historical development of something / very basic or unsophisticated in terms of comfort, convenience, or efficiency.

Prophet : A person regarded as an inspired teacher or proclaimer of the will of God.

Prosperity : The state of being successful and having a lot of money.

Preservation : The state of being preserved, especially to a specified degree.

Philosophy : The study of the fundamental nature of knowledge, reality, and existence, especially when considered as an academic discipline.

Piercingly : Loud or shrill, as the quality of a voice. extremely cold or bitter: a piercing wind.

Photosynthesis : The process by which green plants and some other organisms use sunlight to synthesize nutrients from carbon dioxide and water. Photosynthesis in plants generally involves the green pigment chlorophyll and generates oxygen as a by-product.

Portrays : Describe (someone or something) in a particular way

Possession : The state of having, owning, or controlling something / something that is owned or possessed.

Precipitation : The action or process of precipitating a substance from a solution / rain, snow, sleet, or hail that falls to or condenses on the ground.

Predator : An animal that naturally preys on others / a person who ruthlessly exploits others.

Predominant : Having or exerting control or power / present as the strongest or main element.

Primitive : Relating to, denoting, or preserving the character of an early stage in the evolutionary or historical development of something / very basic or unsophisticated in terms of comfort, convenience, or efficiency.

R

Radiation : The emission of energy as electromagnetic waves or as moving subatomic particles, especially high-energy particles which cause ionization / divergence out from a central point, in particular evolution from an ancestral animal or plant group into a variety of new forms.

Radiological : Relating to the science of X-rays and other high-energy radiation.

Radionuclide's : A radionuclide (radioactive nuclide, radioisotope or radioactive isotope) is an atom that has excess nuclear energy, making it unstable. This excess energy can be used in one of three ways: emitted from the nucleus as gamma radiation; transferred to one of its electrons to release it as a conversion electron; or used to create and emit a new particle (alpha particle or beta particle) from the nucleus.

Rapacious : Aggressively greedy or grasping.

Rebellions : The action or process of resisting authority, control, or convention.

Reckoned : Establish by calculation / be of the opinion.

Redemption : The action of saving or being saved from sin, error, or evil / the action of regaining or gaining possession of something in exchange for payment, or clearing a debt.

Refrain : Stop oneself from doing something.

Renounce : Formally declare one's abandonment of (a claim, right, or possession) / Refuse or resign a right or position, especially one as an heir or trustee / Refuse to continue to recognize or abide by.

Renunciation : The formal rejection of something, typically a belief, claim, or course of action.

Renewable : (of a contract, agreement, etc.) Capable of being renewed / (of a natural resource or source of energy) not depleted when used.

Resurrection : (in Christian belief) The rising of Christ from the dead / (in Christian belief) the rising of the dead at the Last Judgement.

Revered : Feel deep respect or admiration for (something).

Reverent : Feeling or showing deep and solemn respect.

Reverence : Deep respect for someone or something.

Reverential : Of the nature of, due to, or characterized by reverence.

Revelation : A surprising and previously unknown fact that has been disclosed to others / the divine or supernatural disclosure to humans of something relating to human existence.

Rhythms : A strong, regular repeated pattern of movement or sound / the measured flow of words and phrases in verse or prose as determined by the relation of long and short or stressed and unstressed syllables.

Rituals : A prescribed order for performing a ritual ceremony, especially one characteristic of a particular religion or Church / a series of actions or type of behaviour regularly and invariably followed by someone.

Rta : In the vedic religion, Rta is the principle of natural order which regulates and coordinates the operation of the universe and everything within it. In the hymns of the Vedas, Ṛta is described as that which is ultimately responsible for the proper functioning of the natural, moral and sacrificial orders.

S

Sacred : Connected with God or a god or dedicated to a religious purpose and so deserving veneration / religious rather than secular / (of writing or text) embodying the laws or doctrines of a religion.

Sacrificial : Relating to or constituting a sacrifice (Sacrifice mean an act of slaughtering an animal or person or surrendering a possession as an offering to a deity).

Sapiens : Relating to, or being recent humans (Homo sapiens) as distinguished from various fossil hominids.

Scripture : The sacred writings of a religion.

Sclerosis : Abnormal hardening of body tissue / excessive resistance to Change.

Sediment : Matter that settles to the bottom of a liquid; dregs / Sediment is a naturally occurring material that is broken down by processes of weathering and erosion, and is subsequently transported by the action of wind, water, or ice, and/or by the force of gravity acting on the particles.

Serenity : The state of being calm, peaceful, and untroubled.

Semi-arid : A semi-arid climate or steppe climate is the climate of a region that receives precipitation below potential evapotranspiration, but not as low as a desert climate. There are different kinds of semi-arid climates, depending on variables such as temperature, and they give rise to different biomes.

Sentient : Able to perceive or feel things.

Sewage : Waste water and excrement conveyed in sewers.

Shevat : (in the Jewish calendar) The fifth month of the civil and eleventh of the religious year, usually coinciding with parts of January and February.

Significance : The quality of being worthy of attention; importance / the meaning to be found in words or events.

Slaughtered : Extremely drunk.

Smithies : A blacksmith's workshop; a forge.

Solidarity : Unity or agreement of feeling or action, especially among individuals with a common interest; mutual support within a group.

Sovereignty : Supreme power or authority / the authority of a state to govern itself or another state / a self-governing state.

Species : A group of living organisms consisting of similar individuals capable of exchanging genes or interbreeding. The species is the principal natural taxonomic unit, ranking below a genus and denoted by a Latin binomial, e.g. Homo sapiens.

Spiritual : Relating to or affecting the human spirit or soul as opposed to material or physical things / relating to religion or religious belief.

Stewardship : The job of supervising or taking care of something, such as an organization or property

Subdue : Overcome, quieten, or bring under control (a feeling or person).

Subservient : Prepared to obey others unquestioningly.

Sustainable : Able to be maintained at a certain rate or level / able to be upheld or defended.

Sustenance : Food and drink regarded as a source of strength; nourishment / the maintaining of someone or something in life or existence.

T

Theologies : The study of the nature of God and religious belief.

Threatening : Having a hostile or deliberately frightening quality or Manner.

Threshing : Separate grain from (corn or other crops), typically with a flail or by the action of a revolving mechanism / move violently; thrash.

Torah : (in Judaism) The law of God as revealed to Moses and recorded in the first five books of the Hebrew scriptures (the Pentateuch).

Toxicants : A toxic substance introduced into the environment, e.g. a pesticide

Triune : Consisting of three in one (used especially with reference to the Trinity)

Tundra : A vast, flat, treeless Arctic region of Europe, Asia, and North America in which the subsoil is permanently frozen.

Turbidity : Turbidity is the cloudiness or haziness of a fluid caused by large numbers of individual particles that are generally invisible to the naked eye, similar to smoke in air. The measurement of turbidity is a key test of water quality.

U

Ultraviolet :	(of electromagnetic radiation) Having a wavelength shorter than that of the violet end of the visible spectrum but longer than that of X-rays.
Unbridled :	Uncontrolled; Unconstrained.
Universe :	All existing matter and space considered as a whole; the cosmos. The universe is believed to be at least 10 billion light years in diameter and contains a vast number of galaxies; it has been expanding since its creation in the Big Bang about 13 billion years ago.

V

Virtues :	Behaviour showing high moral standards.
Vista :	A pleasing view.

W

Worship :	The feeling or expression of reverence and adoration for a deity

****

REFERENCES

[01] Anurag Tripathi, Deeksha Dave and P.Udaya Bhaskar, (Environmental studies) Preamble for environment and Religion.

[02]. Anurag Tripathi, Religion and Environment

[03]. http:// library. Think quest, org/global warming. htm. & Anurag Tripathi, Dr.k.Raghavan nambiar for environment and ancient India.

[04] Anurag Tripathi, Hindu Mythology and Environment Protection.

[05] Susan M.Darlington, Buddhism.

[06] Ontario Consultants, Jainism and Sikhism Environmental Protection.

[07] Viswa Mohan Tiwari, Islamic Mythology.

[08] Elijah Muhammad, Islamic mythology.

[09] John C.Bergstorm, Christianity.

[10]. www.eartharthcool.com.

[11]. www.google.com.

[12]. www.islam relgion.com.

[13]. Acid Rain, Environment Protection agency August 6 2002.

[14]. K.V.S.G. Murali Krishna, Environmental studies.

[15] www.bbc.co.uk › ... › Religion, science and the environment

[16] [Christopher Key ChappleLoyola Marymount University published by The Forum on Religion and Ecology]

[17] Larry west, about.com

[18] Ven. Sheng-yen (08/31/2000 working session on environmental protection at theWaldorf-AstoriaHotel.

[19]Triratna Mananadhar"SaddhammaKovida

[20] "Ven. K. Sri Dhammananda - Daily Buddhist Devotions,(Kualalampur: Buddhist Missionary Society, 1993), P 96

[21] Green Faith Webinar with Dr. Stephanie Kaza University of Vermont March19.(2012)[Buddha's statue with tree]

[22] Origin of Environmental Science From Vedas----Shashi Tiwari

[23] Environmental Conservation and Indian Consciousness - Rajendra Singh , Tarun Bharat Sangh, 2004

[24] Yajurvedic Declarations of Human RightsDr.Manmohan Acharya

[25] The Vedic way to preserving environment - Vaishnavi Sanoj

[26] Indian Environmental concerns: Protection of Indian Religious and Cultural heritage-Asif Ahmed

[27] A Contemplative Scientific Review From Manusmruti -- S. N. Padhy, S.K. Dash and Ratnaprava Mohapatra.

[28] Our Sacred Earth Hinduism and The Environment---By Matthew McDermott

[29] Manusmriti, the Hindu Law Book: Economic Ideas---Ratan Lal Basu.

[30] Environmental Protection and Water Reverence in Ancient Indian CultureK.N. SharmaSecretary, International Commission on Irrigation and Drainage (ICID)48, Nyaya Marg, Chanakyapuri, New Delhi – 110 021, India

[31] www.interfaithdeclaration.org.

[32] Sharing Time: Reverence for Creation -- by Karen Ashton.

[33] Ancient Indian History and Culture - By Chidambara Kulkarni Orient Longman Ltd. 1974. 34. Environmental ethics in the Hindu Vedas and Puranas in IndiaR. Renugadevi (Department of History, Annamalai University, Annamalainagar-608002.Tamilnadu, India

[35] Christians and the Environment – Author: Alan Marshall – December 1998 (with revisions to October 2005)

[36]The impact ofEnvironmentalEthics on Christian Ethics Kevin Cowtan29th April 2006.

[37] Environmental Ethics and Christian Theology-- Willis Jenkins.

[38] www.lung.org

[39]Economictimes.indiatimes.com/articleshow/65460499.cms?utm_sourcecontentofinterest &utm medium text &utm campaign cppst

[40] "Bhopal trial: Eight convicted over India gas disaster". BBC News. 7 June 2010. Archived from the original on 7 June 2010. Retrieved 7 June 2010

[41] Madhya Pradesh Government : Bhopal Gas Tragedy Relief and Rehabilitation Department, Bhopal". Mp.gov.in. Archived from the original on 18 May 2012. Retrieved 28 August 2012.

[42] http://www.theweathernetwork.com/uk/news/articles/indias-deadly-heatwave-nears-end-as-monsoon-arrives/52420/

[43] Chernobyl at 25th anniversary – Frequently Asked Questions – April 2011" (PDF). World Health Organisation. 23 April 2011. Retrieved 14 April 2012

[44]https://www.researchgate.net/publication/257816315AirPollution in Bangalore, India A Six-Year Trend and Health Implication Analysis [accessed Oct 08 2018].

****